Mary Evans · Sarah Moore
Hazel Johnstone

Detecting the Social

Order and Disorder in Post-1970s Detective Fiction

G000254923

palgrave
macmillan

Mary Evans
Department of Gender Studies
London School of Economics and Political
  Science
London, UK

Hazel Johnstone
Department of Gender Studies
London School of Economics and Political
  Science
London, UK

Sarah Moore
Department of Social & Policy Sciences
University of Bath
Bath, UK

ISBN 978-3-319-94519-4   ISBN 978-3-319-94520-0   (eBook)
https://doi.org/10.1007/978-3-319-94520-0

Library of Congress Control Number: 2018947626

Cover image: © Michael Kemp/Alamy Stock Photo
Cover design by Fatima Jamadar

This Palgrave Macmillan imprint is published by the registered company Springer Nature Switzerland AG
The registered company address is: Gewerbestrasse 11, 6330 Cham, Switzerland

Acknowledgements

There are many people whom we would like to thank, not least of all the many inspiring authors of detective fiction. We hope that they, and their works, will continue to flourish. We would also like to say how much these authors have contributed to hours of rewarding reading. Given that detective fiction does not explore the happiest of human situations it has nevertheless invariably contributed to the understanding of human actions.

Other people have given us help of different kinds. Our thanks go to the organisers of conferences in Edinburgh and Iceland (Sarah Arens and Stacy Gillis respectively) and to Fiona Peters for the work she has done in the past five years for organising the Captivating Criminality conferences. These meetings now attract both academics and the writers of detective fiction and are a major resource for anyone wishing to talk and think about the subject of detection. We are deeply grateful for the help of Ralph Kinnear in helping to check and edit the draft manuscript.

Many individuals have given us recommendations about what we should, and should not, read. Here we should like to thank in particular Kathy Davis, Sadie Wearing, Diana Lindsay, Adam Burgess, and Judy Wright.

Finally, we would like to thank our colleague and fellow reader Hazel Johnstone for all that she has done to make this book possible. Not only does Hazel have encyclopaedic knowledge of, and faultless judgement about, detective fiction, she also has been a consistent support and encouragement throughout the writing of this book.

Mary Evans
Sarah Moore

Contents

Contents

1

Introduction

Who, Why and How

Collecting material for a book about detective fiction is a project somewhat akin to counting the grains of sand on a beach. This genre of fiction is so extensive and so widely read that anyone who has ever ventured to speak or write about it has always been instantly reminded that they have excluded and overlooked yet another author. Everyone has a favourite writer of detective fiction. Careful readers (indeed those who have already acquired skills in detection) will have noticed that we are already speaking of detective, rather than crime fiction. The term is often used inter-changeably but here the term will be that of detective fiction. The reasons for this are twofold: first that crime does not necessarily involve the death of individual human beings. Indeed, what might be defined as crime in the early decades of the twenty-first century is often entirely conducted at a distance from any form of human interaction: cyber-crime, identity theft, criminal forms of the exchange and transfer of money can all be conducted from any location and directed towards untold others. The human consequences of this form of crime are often dramatic: pensioners, for example, might—and indeed

© The Author(s) 2019
M. Evans et al., *Detecting the Social*, https://doi.org/10.1007/978-3-319-94520-0_1

sometimes do—lose their hopes of financial support and security in old age, but they are not literally killed. To many people this might suggest a somewhat artificial or meaningless distinction, but this study will maintain the consistent tradition of detective fiction which has always involved the actual loss of human life, through a determined human action. This does not mean that the guilty have always been either apprehended or punished; detection is, as De Quincey pointed out at the beginning of the nineteenth century, a very fine art but not always one with entirely predictable outcomes.[1]

The second reason for maintaining the term detective, rather than crime, fiction is that in using this term we make explicit that process of detecting which we regard as central to this study. As one of the characters says in Anthony Horowitz's *The Word is Murder*:

> They're not called murder victim stories. They're not called Criminal stories. They're called detective stories.[2]

How to detect, what to look for, what to regard as reliable or unreliable evidence are all part not just of detection in fiction but of every form of research, be it in the social sciences, the humanities or the natural sciences. We cannot find out anything that we need to know unless we have some certainty about how we will proceed. And what detective fiction has done, from its very earliest years is to offer some diverse possibilities about how to find out what is going on in the world. Detective fiction, certainly at its best, encourages us to think and more particularly to think about what is going on in the world around us. Again, at its best, it asks us to pose questions about why individuals are behaving in the way that they do and to engage in the work of moral arbitration rather than moral judgement. Perhaps most of all it does not ask us to judge others, often a conventional expectation of much mainstream fiction. Read the notes for reading groups provided at the back of many of novels and readers will find questions to ask about what s/he 'should' have done. The long arm of the literary critic F. R. Leavis continues to stretch across swathes of fiction; surrounding readers (and writers) with the endless expectation of the acceptance of moral certainty. Detectives, be they Sherlock Holmes, Lord Peter Wimsey, Miss Jane Marple or their later incarnations in the form of Lisbeth Salander and Harry Hole, do not, however, accept the world as it is put before them. Nor, and this is very much part of the appeal of detective fiction, do they accept the given social order as a source of moral virtue and behaviour. It is not that this form of often quiet and overlooked radicalism is an attribute only of detective fiction—some canonical British fiction shares aspects of this characteristic—but it is a rejection of the normative acceptance that many societies expect of their citizens. Not the least of this expectation is what can be described as the 'aspirational coercion' that has accompanied the normalisation of neo-liberalism: the idea that we all have the same social 'wants' and are prepared, and expected, to work in highly individualised ways to secure these ends. So, dissent, marginality and often explicit disagreement are often part and parcel of the make-up of the very best detectives. Holmes and his later colleagues do not naturally accept authority or the given normative order; they may live what can be labelled as conventional lives, but these chosen ways of individual life should not be assumed to indicate a wholesale acceptance of the boundaries and judgments of the given social order.

We are therefore proposing here, first, that detective fiction has a complex and important relationship to both the social and the epistemological order of contemporary western societies. Second, we shall argue that the appeal and the importance of detective fiction (and the reason for its considerable popularity) is that it is concerned with the life, and the problems of that life, that people living in the west encounter, either as fact or in terms of worries, concerns and fantasies about that world. These sentences make explicit the geographical and historical location of the literature that we have chosen to investigate; the detective fiction of Europe in the period after 1970. In this period, much of Europe has experienced considerable legal and social change; sometimes widely welcomed but increasingly—in the second decade of the twenty-first century—leading to politics that have revived supposedly extinct forms of nationalism. The citizens of this new Europe read more detective fiction than other form of fiction. Anyone who reads detective fiction will be aware that detective fiction is now not only the most widely read genre of literature on the planet but is also a global form, written by citizens of diverse countries and cultures and situated within similarly widely different contexts, both chronological and geographical. Detection and detectives have been situated, for example, in fourteenth century England, Nazi Germany, pre-revolutionary Russia and most decades of the twentieth century. Amongst these books are those which—for example the novels of Boris Akunin set in late nineteenth century Moscow—illuminate much about those societies. Thus, Akunin paints a picture of pre-revolutionary Moscow as a sophisticated city with a functioning and competent bureaucracy.[3] Detectives have also come in a range of genders and races, with many (albeit largely white) women becoming iconic figures in the genre. To a certain extent the entry of considerable numbers of women into detection in the second half of the twentieth century has been much encouraged by the opening of employment for women in the police forces of various countries in the second half of the twentieth century. But before this, the tradition of the amateur detective had allowed the iconic figure of Miss Jane Marple to emerge in the works of Agatha Christie. This apparently quiet and conservative figure interrupted (and continues to interrupt) all expectations of that heavily defended persona, in both emotional and literal terms, of the male detective. Nor was she alone. At the same time as Christie was letting loose the quietly subversive intelligence of Miss Jane Marple her contemporary Gladys Mitchell was demonstrating, through her central figure Mrs Bradley, the possibilities of psychoanalysis in understanding those aspects of human action and motivation which resulted in murder; a very different account of the motives for murder which led Mitchell to write parodies of Christie.[4] Detective fiction, in the hands of these women, was not about maintaining the political and intellectual orthodoxies of the first decades of the twentieth century. In the latter decades of the twentieth century various 'girls with guns' took their places in detective fiction but even these figures, the creations of, for example, Sue Grafton and Sarah Paretsky, owed a considerable amount to Miss Marple and other women writers of the so-called 'Golden Age' of British detective fiction. Grafton and Paretsky are both writing about the United States but what they contribute to is an aspect of 'Golden Age' fiction—that of the amateur female detective—which has been less present in the latter years of the twentieth century in the UK and Europe.[5] Yet the legacy of the 'Golden Age' is to be found in the validation of intuition, the 'reading' of body language and the refusal to accept with unquestioning obedience the words of powerful men.

Thus, the gender of detective fiction has shown itself to be, certainly in the twentieth century, an open space for both male and female writers and male and female protagonists. But two things have changed very little. The first is that the race of the detective, and certainly in the detective fiction of Europe since 1970 which is considered here, has changed little over the decades. It remains the case that the great majority of detectives, of whatever gender, are white. What we might make of this is an issue to be explored later in this book; here it is sufficient to comment that this singularity of racial identity in detection encourages us to recognise that to a very significant extent western societies are not just ruled by white men but are also policed by them. The idea that detection might cross racial lines—that the socially rather than the individually marginal person might investigate the powerful—still remains to be explored in detective fiction. The second aspect of the identity of the detective that has remained stable is that of their sexual identity; largely, although not exclusively heterosexual. What has changed, and certainly since the days of Lord Peter Wimsey and Miss Marple, is the form of sexual relationships in which detectives are involved: heterosexual monogamy is no longer an assumed basis for sexual relations. The aspiration persists amongst some contemporary characters, the realisation is rather more infrequent.

These changes, and lack of changes, demonstrate the way in which detective fiction has implicitly recorded much of the reality of both social change and its absence in Europe in the past fifty years. In terms of significant change, the 1970s, across Europe, were years in which much of that continent tore up its legal framework about the intimate lives of its citizens. It was not that the final decades of the twentieth century invented new forms of sexuality but what did emerge was a new public discussion of human diversity. On matters of divorce, the decriminalisation of homosexuality, reproductive rights, the legal autonomy of women and laws about the organisation of marriage, nation states changed the legal framework of the personal lives of their citizens. All of these changes are reflected in detective fiction. But what did not change, and thus the emphasis above of the race and the sexuality of detectives, was what can be described as the 'hidden' face of power in most European societies. Across these countries, despite the new liberality and apparent inclusiveness of statute, white, heterosexual men dominated positions of power. Those in these positions of power enacted policies which often supported policies about crime and punishment which continued to impinge more severely on those of marginalised communities. Thus, for example, the changes in laws about discrimination on matters of race in the UK have occurred at the same time as rates of imprisonment for young black men are significantly higher than those of their white compatriots. In the United States, policies about the punishment of crime (specifically those related to drug offences) have resulted in what is being widely described as the incarceration of the young black, male, population.[6] What this example suggests is one of the forms of social fracture within the twenty-first century: societies with various forms of liberal legislation in which elites drawn from traditional contexts of class, gender and race variously continue to operate and implicitly endorse conventional stereotypes.

The recognition of this persistence of various forms of social inequality—across those three foundational social variables of class, race and gender—runs through detective fiction in the years after 1970. It is not, however, the case that this volume includes detective fiction from all parts of Europe although the genre is widely read throughout the area. The concentration here is on those Nordic countries and the United Kingdom where 'noir' as a form of detective fiction has become most apparent. This is not, we shall argue, a matter of distinct literary traditions but because of the particular set of political circumstances in these countries: namely the emergence of scepticism about post Second World War political settlements, specifically that of the legitimacy of state provided forms of welfare provision within liberal democracies. Those countries which have now become part of the EU (for example Poland) had similar regimes, but within very different political forms. In what is regarded as 'western' Europe countries such as Greece, Italy, Germany and Spain all faced different political challenges, not the least that of coming to terms with their various departures from conventional democratic forms. France remains as a country with a long and energetic tradition of detective fiction but relatively little of that work—with the obvious exception of the French speaking, Belgian born George Simenon—has been translated into English. Despite the general focus on Scandinavia and the UK readers will see that novels from France and the Republic of Ireland appear later in this text.

The date of 1970 is taken as the starting point for this study because it was at the beginning of that decade that the social changes around individual rights coincided with an increasing abandonment of the shared political assumptions that had ensured something of a consensus about the central role of the state in the support of the lives of its citizens. In short, as many other studies have pointed out, what was at first an economic theory supporting the defining role that the market should play in the working of the economy gradually became a more general social theory, usually described as 'neo-liberalism', in which individuals were assumed to have full responsibility for their circumstances. In the UK for example, the post Second World War 'settlement' of the implementation of much of the Beveridge Report of 1942 was increasingly debated. In the years after 1979, when Margaret Thatcher became Prime Minister of the UK, neo-liberal ideas became a defining aspect of contests about the nature and the future of the British Welfare State.[7] A similar contest was to be played out across much of Europe, particularly in Scandinavian countries where the aspirations and the empirical reach of the welfare state had been greater than in other parts of Europe. This central political issue plays a very considerable part in the detective fiction of much of northern Europe, distinctively more so than in countries of the so-called 'south' (Italy, Spain, Portugal and Greece) where questions of the integration of organised crime with the criminal justice system play a more conspicuous part.

Detective fiction did not, as a genre, take up a single, simple, position in terms of this emergent politics. But what it did do was to put before its readers a number of issues which were central to anyone living in Europe. The first of these was to revive the question of the moral legitimacy of both the law and policing. Those questions were also asked in what became known as the 'new criminology' of the 1970s.[8] In the work of various authors old assumptions about the 'causes' of crime were thrown aside in favour of a discussion of the ways in which definitions of crime were created, and very often created in the interests of the rich rather than the poor.[9] The second question asked was even wider: to ask whether or not the form of society, the very values of society, were those which were worth defending. In this, the public moral plurality introduced by reforming legislation about the personal lives of citizens opened up new debates in which words such as 'patriarchy' became central. Although it was not until 1989 that the politics of the Soviet Union (and its satellite states) were transformed, the binary between capitalism and socialism diminished; leaving in its wake a politics in which the citizen became increasingly individualised and with rights to what was constructed as 'choice' and personal freedom. At the same time as those definitions were extended so it also became increasingly apparent, as forms of financial de-regulation came to transform economic life, a tiny number of individuals could become very rich and—crucially—distant from most forms of legal jurisdiction. The third—and a matter of considerable separation between Europe and the United States—was that of the state's attitude to policing and issues of crime and punishment. The power of the view that individuals chose to commit crime—dominant in much of the rhetoric around crime in the US—was countered in Europe by a more nuanced view typified by what Tony Blair was to describe as the 'causes of crime.' This difference, much enhanced by the political importance attached in the United States to the right of citizens to carry guns, has created differences in policing, and detection, which are evident in the detective fiction of the USA and Europe. Nobody who has walked around a European city in the past fifteen years is still able to assume that the police forces of many European countries are not armed, but the difference is that the citizens of these countries are seldom allowed—legally—to carry arms. What this creates is a situation in which the expectation, however fictional, is that the police will proceed in their work by forms of traditional procedural methods. The 'perps', so central to the fiction of many writers of detective fiction set in the United States, the people who die in armed exchanges with the police or private detectives are less common in European literature. The language of detective fiction in which suspects are 'taken out' is indicative of some of the differences between the United States, a country where the public ownership of guns is fiercely defended, and Europe. In the light of these various issues, all of which revolve around the questions of what constitutes justice and how we define the criminal, the individual citizen might well come to ask the question of what exactly is going on and how we might begin both to define and challenge those terms.

These comments set out some of the context in which the detective fiction in the period after 1970 is based. But whilst definition of, and information about, the political and social circumstances of these years can be gleaned from numerous studies there is little available guidance about how to study detective fiction itself. Literary critics as well as those from the social sciences have used detective fiction to illustrate social themes and there are numerous studies of the many distinguished writers of detective fiction in the past two hundred years. This study, however, is attempting to look at more than individual authors. Indeed, its purpose is to look at the work of a great many authors over a period of almost fifty years. So, this study does not intend to use detective fiction as a form of data which can provide illustration of the social world. There will certainly be suggestions about the congruence of the themes and the resolutions within detective fiction with those of the real world, but this is not intended as an exercise in collecting instances of similarity between events in the social world and fiction. It is intended, in the best sense of the work of the detective, as an investigation. In this, there may well be the discovery of 'clues' (those points of similarity between the real and the fictional world) but more importantly it is hoped to define coherent patterns of understanding and explanation of how the world of the late twentieth and early twentieth century works. The detective fiction of Europe since 1970 we would argue is collectively an argument about the Politics/politics—both of the private and the public space—of that world. Very little mainstream fiction, we would argue, has attempted to understand this world; indeed, the traditions of canonical fiction have been largely maintained.

The guidelines—the procedural rules of this study—are these: that the texts chosen are from Europe, a term which includes the United Kingdom and the Republic of Ireland. Whatever the current political battles around the relationship of the UK to the European Union, as far as this book is concerned the UK is part of Europe and will continue to be so whatever the outcome of Brexit. The decision not to include the United States and other parts of the globe is that the canvas would then become both too wide and face complex questions about the export of literary traditions and the political and intellectual baggage which those traditions carry. The choice of texts is based both on the choice of the public—in that many of the most popular writers of detective fiction are included—and the judgments of the considerable number of associations awarding excellence in the writing of detective fiction. We can note that the genre of both crime and detective fiction is one which has an organised and influential institutional life. There are awards for good and outstanding writing, well attended annual conferences and—to judge from many of the fulsome acknowledgments by many authors—a supportive community. Since thanks to other authors are seldom to be found in mainstream fiction it is worth pointing out that whatever else are the differences within the pages of crime and detective fiction its authors have a strong sense of shared purpose.[10]

That camaraderie, the sense of strong working relationships between people, has also often been mentioned as part of the police force. The 'partners' of crime (the Holmes/Watson tradition which has continued into, for example, the Morse/Lewis relationship in the novels of Colin Dexter) speaks of those very powerful partnerships forged through long working hours, an often-hostile bureaucracy, and, most recently and perhaps most importantly, that sense of the police force standing at an inter-section of criminal life and the workings of the law. As increasing numbers of detective novels have demonstrated, the police might well catch villains—know exactly who 'did it'—but bringing a successful prosecution against that individual poses often difficult and intractable problems. This inter-section of European legal systems and the institutions of policing is one which has increasingly come under scrutiny in both detective fiction and in reality. Members of the police—in fiction and reality—are frustrated by the decisions of the courts; the courts and other public institutions are equally frustrated by police failures of investigation, arising from reasons of incompetence and/or corruption. The 'law' as the written embodiment of a society's expectations and aspirations can, in these circumstances, become either the impediment to justice or the basis of hopes for its realisation.

One work of non-fiction which illustrates the issue of the relationship between law and the practice of policing particularly well is a book of non-fiction by an ex-policeman, Stephen Fulcher, called *Catching a Serial Killer*.[11] Serial killers, as any student of crime fiction or actual crime figures knows, are very rare, however much they loom large in the public imagination. Fulcher's book concerns his work, when a Detective Superintendent for the Wiltshire Police Force in tracking down the person who had murdered two young women. But the book is also an education in the work of the police in the contemporary UK, not least because it refers to much of the technological and legal apparatus of modern policing. In the case of the former the technology helped to identify the killer, but in the latter—as we will see—the legal requirements about the circumstances of a person's confession radically undermined the conduct of the case. Students of both crime and detective fiction (in print and in film) may be familiar with the initials SIO and DNA, others may be less aware of the agencies and the technology obscured by other initials such as TRL, VODS, POLSA, PACE, IPCC, SCAS, PCMH, HOLMES, MIR, PNC, APNR and TIE.[12] The extent of this list demonstrates that the years of policing through conversations, with the tools of a notebook and a pen are becoming rare in reality, however much they may appear in fiction. But what it also demonstrates is that 'police procedural' novels as they have been defined increasingly include ever changing and developing forms of technology. All police work and all forms of detection have always involved some form of systematic work—the elimination of suspects and the collecting of alibis for example—but what has emerged since 1970 is a highly complex mix of both technological expertise and entirely conventional forms of interrogation. That complexity is illustrated both in reality— the particular case which Fulcher discusses—and in the novels of Maj Sjöwall and Per Wahlöö in which Martin Beck is the central character. As the back cover of one of these novels, *The Man on the Balcony*, says 'The dedicated work of the police seems to be leading nowhere… But then Beck remembers someone - or something - he overheard…'[13] Little could be more in the tradition of Agatha Christie and Miss Jane Marple than such a serendipitous event; precisely the recognition that an acute awareness of human speech and behaviour is central to identifying those suspected of crime. Fulcher worked, like Martin Beck, with all the machinery of late twentieth century at his disposal. But at the same time his final identification of the murderer came through conversation, albeit in his case a conversation held in the wrong place and outside legal requirements. Nevertheless, that tracking of the suspect, came about through that mix of the use of technology and the traditional methods of police procedure with human acuity which had aided Martin Beck. What these instances—one fictional and the other non-fictional suggest—is that uneasy contemporary relationship between formal procedure and 'expert' advice and what is sometimes described as 'common' sense. The limits of that 'common' sense have been made clear in numerous instances of, for example the stereotyping of criminals, but much detective fiction retains a considerable sympathy for the idea, if not for 'common' sense, then at least a place for the intuitive and happenstance.

This possibility was, as suggested, not available to Fulcher. His identification of the murderer was initially made possible by a very simple form of technology, the APNR, which stands for Automatic Plate Number Recognition. Far more problematic was PACE, the 1984 Police and Criminal Evidence Act, which led to the dismissal of Fulcher for gross misconduct. What this seemed to embody for Fulcher—and it is important to remember here that he is writing from the point of view of the police rather than the accused—is the emphasis which the Act placed on what is named in detective fiction as the narrative of the 'police procedural'. In this narrative Fulcher suggests, all the criminal has to do to escape being caught and punished is to learn the rules of the criminal game. This may take the form of those elementary precautions of never leaving fingerprints or traces of DNA to the more sophisticated evasions of laws practised in forms of cybercrime. As Fulcher wrote of the workings of the 1984 Act:

> Bear in mind that if a criminal is any good, the only source of information is reposed in the perpetrator's mind. Yet PACE means it's the one area detectives can't go. There is an endemic problem with PACE that prevents voluntary confessions being accepted - because everything about it, from the right to silence to the right to a lawyer who will actively stop

you from incriminating yourself, is engineered so that criminals don't cough. Since PACE was introduced it has essentially blocked off interviewing suspects as an investigative avenue. As such modern policing has become a passive, box-ticking exercise, with coppers picking up the clues a careless criminal has left behind. A trained monkey could do it; you don't need a detective. It means, evidently, that coppers will only ever catch clumsy criminals.[14]

This view is, of course, that of a senior policeman who lost his job because he had received the confession of a suspect outside the confines of a police station and the formalities of an interview. When the suspect subsequently refused to sign the confession the case for the defence argued that the suspect had been interviewed outside the PACE code. The process which examined Fulcher's case, its implications for him and the many legal arguments surrounding it, occupy more than half of his book and in this part of the narrative yet another crucial institution occurs: the IPCC or Independent Police Complaints Committee, which in this context appears to be antagonistic towards Fulcher. What is made clear in the second part of Fulcher's book—the part when the murderer has been found—is the complexity of the contemporary relationship between the police and the legal system. Fulcher tells of a situation in which the murderer is caught by a relatively simple piece of technology; no intensive investigation is needed to demonstrate that the guilty person was in the car in the right place at the right time. That person then confesses, in very large part because a rapport has been established between the detective and the suspect. But the confession is without legal weight because when the suspect, a man whom we all now know is the murderer, is taken into custody, interviewed in the police station, under oath, with a solicitor present and a full record being made of the proceedings, he refuses to say anything. Fulcher's murderer, like that of the villains who haunt the pages of much contemporary fiction, can be identified but they cannot be effectively prosecuted in courts of law. A fictional instance of the same issues is the character Cafferty, the *bête noire* of the Rebus novels by Ian Rankin. Cafferty is always transparently—to Rebus and the reader—the guilty party. But there are many occasions on which Cafferty's access to clever and well-connected lawyers means he thwarts Rebus in his attempts to put him behind bars. It is not, in the case of Rebus, England's Crime Prosecution Service that is so fearful of failed prosecution but the similar processes and institutions of Scotland. Across the UK all police forces are bound by strict expectations that cases will 'stand up in court'. Rebus, like other fictional detectives, is well aware of the public expectations that the police will 'catch' criminals; he is equally aware, as many members of the public are not, that he is often powerless to charge or punish them. But perhaps quite as much as the ongoing issue of the distance between known illegality and effective prosecution is the wider issue of the gap between technological expertise and material collected by forms of surveillance and human observation and understanding. What is raised by Fulcher, as it is by Ian Rankin and others, is the question of the agency and indeed the authority of the human subject; the question endlessly explored in discussions of the part that human judgement will play in societies that are increasingly dependent on technological expertise.[15]

So, the example explored in Fulcher's book, where a criminal is known but only prosecuted, if at all, with great difficulty has created new kinds of challenges in both fiction and reality for the apprehension and the punishment of criminals. This of course, again in both kinds of contexts, creates new kinds of police work and new forms of relevant competence. These new challenges were not, it has to be said, derived from reforms instigated by the police but in large part because of three infamous instances in the English courts and police systems of the miscarriage of justice: the cases of the prosecutions and subsequent imprisonment of the Guildford Four and the Birmingham Six (both in 1975) and the Maguire Seven in 1976. All these cases related to bomb attacks in England, part of the IRA campaign against the UK's policies in Northern Ireland. Every one of the people originally charged in these cases later had their convictions over-turned in 1989, but not before some of those convicted (for example in the case of the Guildford Four) had served prison sentences of fifteen years. It was revealed in the appeals against these notoriously 'unsafe' convictions that the police had extracted confessions through torture as well as other—subsequently disallowed—forms of interrogation. When the 1984 Police and

Criminal Evidence Act was passed it was in part in answer to criticism of the police methods employed in these cases but also because it was becoming increasingly obvious that the police force was losing significant public support and legitimacy. The extent of this emerging distance between the police and its public credibility is suggested by the fact that the Act was passed during the years when the Conservative Party led by Margaret Thatcher was in power, a political leader and party with longstanding and uncritical support for the police. Nevertheless, vocal pressure groups and significant groups in the legal profession had led campaigns to raise awareness about the often highly partial workings of the law. Amongst that partiality campaigns had identified—and continue to identify—examples such as the 'stop and search laws' which impacted on the African-Caribbean population and the consistent failure to prosecute accusations of rape and sexual violence. In all these contexts, amongst which the abject failure of the London Metropolitan Police to investigate effectively the murder of the teenager Stephen Lawrence in 1993, was perhaps the most notorious, what was becoming increasingly apparent to many people was that 'the law' in the form of both the police force and the criminal justice system had a somewhat blinkered attitude to the identification and the prosecution of criminals. The Lawrence case, and the public disquiet about the police conduct, resulted in the judgement of the 1999 Macpherson Report of 'institutional racism' in the Metropolitan Police.[16]

The Macpherson Report was only instigated after a concerted press and public campaign about one specific murder. But what had been gathering strength throughout the 1980s was a recognition of the corrupt and brutal possibilities of police work; possibilities which had been more than realised in the UK in the cases involving not just the politics of Northern Ireland but also in those politics resultant from the Hillsborough Football Stadium loss of life in 1989 and the Miners Strike of 1984. The crucial link between all these instances is that of the 'outsider' status imposed on the victims of police corruption; the working class (at home or at leisure) and the Black population are accorded less respect and credibility.[17] Across Europe other instances of corruption and bias were being similarly identified as they have been in novels set in mainland Europe.[18] What has emerged, across Europe is a recognition that police work has to be subject to regular public and external examination. This, in its turn, drives new definitions about what is, and is not, 'legal' since the institution responsible for the keeping of the law is now subjected to that same long arm of 'the law' which the police had at one time been assumed to represent. An uncritical view of the police force has always been tempered by concerns about its intelligence and professional competence, but what becomes a defining factor in the majority of works of detective fiction by the middle of the 1980s is a resultant complex location of moral boundaries. These boundaries no longer coincide easily with the police as 'good' and the criminal as 'bad'. It is not the case that all detectives become infected with the kind of existential doubt about their work which the novels of, for example, Henning Mankell suggest, but that moral certainty of purpose and method is increasingly rare amongst those charged with the keeping of the law.

But just as the ways in which the police work, and in particular the ways in which they collect evidence, have become more constrained by legislation so two other factors, one longstanding and one of more recent origin, have played, and continue to play, a part in the transformation of policing. The first, with a long history, was that of the place of the public voice in the prosecution of actually criminal or socially unacceptable behaviour. The second was the question of the reliability of evidence based in new forms of technology. In the case of the first, there is a long, trans-cultural, history of what has been spoken of as 'people taking the law into their own hands'. This has taken various forms, from the vicious and often murderous actions of the lynch mob to the instances where civil disobedience has challenged both the letter and the implementation of the law. Examples of these kinds of behaviour range from the racially motivated attacks on the African-American citizens of the United States to the vocal and influential campaign fought in the UK to implement what became known as 'Sarah's Law' in England. This law, passed in 2011, was a result of public and media interventions after the murder of eight-year-old Sarah Payne in 2000. The law as passed for England and Wales allowed individual citizens to be informed about convictions for child sexual abuse for any person having contact with children. But it was a law which had disastrous consequences. An entirely innocent Iranian Bijan Ebrahami was murdered as a result of being falsely identified as a paedophile; an equally innocent woman paediatrician was forced from her home after numerous death threats.[19] Against these disastrous consequences of legislation propelled into existence by sensational campaigns about threat and danger there are other, more positive, instances of community and individual resistance to various aspects of the law. These include recent campaigns in London about housing and—perhaps most famously in the past fifty years—the continued forms of civil disobedience against the UK's possession of nuclear weapons.[20] All these various instances, of the law being questioned outside accepted institutions and processes have increasingly been written into the narratives of detective fiction.

So, in an increasingly complex relationship with the public, and powerful media voices, the police also have to contend with political pressures to arrest those suspected of serious crime. This pressure on the police—an issue spoken of widely in detective fiction—has resulted, in reality, in those miscarriages of justice cited earlier. The political rhetoric about the 'terrorists' of the IRA, voiced by Margaret Thatcher at the same time as her government was also seeking ways to negotiate with those same 'terrorists' was nothing new in British politics then or since.[21] But it is important to recognise here that policing is highly attuned to political discourse: pressures from the public, the media and politicians to make sure that the 'guilty' are brought to justice continue to inform both the identification and the prosecution of suspects. Whilst PACE has done much to regulate the ways in which the interrogation of suspects is conducted in England and Wales, what still remains evident is that behaviour towards suspects in police stations can be at best careless and at the worst brutal. The detective novels of William Shaw about police work in London in the 1960s and 1970s are replete with references to 'old' forms of policing, essentially the years before PACE. But a study of the cases of people who have died in police custody in 2017 would suggest that whilst legislation has done much to regulate the interrogation of suspects what it has not been able to do is to eliminate those attitudes to people suspected of crime which result in serious physical harm.[22] Neither has that judgment of 'institutional racism' lost its relevance; the issue of 'joint enterprise', with its mobilisation in some cases of highly racialised ideas of 'gang culture' has recently become another area in which questionable attitudes about race and race relations have been suggested.[23] These questions, about the values and attitudes of both the police force and the public on matters of crime and the prosecution of the criminal have given to many fictional detectives (whether privately or publicly employed) something of the status of the arbiter of moral judge. This continues that tradition of detective fiction, evident across the west in the 1930s and the 1940s, in which the police forces of many countries were viewed both as so stupid and so corrupt that they could always be relied upon to arrest the wrong person for the wrong reasons. Something of that tradition has informed much of the various 'noir' detective fiction of Europe since 1970. There are many loved and highly respected publicly employed police men and women in these works but what these individuals share is that they are—to a man and a woman—at odds not just with the senior figures with whom they work but also with many of the values which those figures embody. Across Europe senior management in detective fiction is represented as self-serving, careerist, greedy, incompetent and corrupt. Not every figure represents every one of these negative traits, but the point that is being made is that which has been made in military history: that campaigns are often fought and won despite the participation of officers.

How we read this is complex: on the one hand this refusal and suspicion of hierarchy could be regarded as an energetic determination to question authority and power. There are various ways of 'speaking truth to power' and detective fiction often chooses to do this by explicit criticism of the powerful. On the other hand, we might argue that to refuse the possibilities of forms of power—and in some cases forms of specialist professional competence—is to come perilously close to that validation of 'common sense' which allows considerable space for prejudice and ignorance. Detective fiction does not resolve this issue but what it does do is to explore a question which has become central to western (if not global) politics: the relationship between power and forms of public action, knowledge and information. In the following pages we examine the ways in which detective fiction has grappled with these, and other issues which are central to the experience of living in the late twentieth and early twenty-first centuries. In the following chapters we both 'set the scene'—which follows immediately in Chapter 2—and then consider some of the key themes and questions of contemporary 'noir' fiction. Two themes have emerged as central in our reading of the novels: that of the question of who's to blame for murder and the issue of the way of life, the very context of our contemporary existence, that results in murder. These are the central themes of Chapters 3 and 4. The final chapter echoes that infamous command, 'Only Connect'. It would be foolish to suppose that we have achieved that Eureka moment of connecting the personal with the social but our first hope is that we have moved towards connecting the social with the powerful imagination of detective fiction.

A second aspiration here is to rectify what we see as absences in current academic writing about detective fiction, notably increased since the beginning of the twenty-first century. So, finally here we turn to consider how our contribution fits alongside this body of literature. Much of this work is focussed on contemporary Scandinavian novels—'Scandi noir', as it's often called—and aims to sketch out the emergence and development of this genre (see, for example, Forshaw 2012), or its translation from novels into film and television (see, for example, Effron 2013; Peacock 2013, 2014). Genre tends to be a key concern in these accounts—that is, ascertaining the parameters of certain types of detective fiction across media—and that reflects the disciplinary backgrounds and interests of those writing on detective fiction today. That is, they tend to belong to Arts or Media Studies disciplines. On occasion, this body of work engages with sociological issues, most notably Gregoriou's linguistic analysis of deviance in detective fiction (2007) and Astrom et al.'s (2012) edited collection on the depiction of rape in Stieg Larsson's Millennium Trilogy. By and large, this sociologically-oriented work concentrates on the key themes, structures, and devices in the fiction studied, and the focus remains on the novels themselves, rather than what they might tell us about the world beyond. More thorough-going sociological accounts are very rare indeed. More accurately, sociological accounts of detective fiction have *become* rare. The German, marxist thinkers of the early and mid-twentieth century realised the value of the detective genre for social theorising. Siegfried

Kracauer, who wrote an (unpublished for decades) manuscript during the early 1920s about the detective novel, saw in the genre a distillation of the central problem of modern social life: the evacuation of meaning from decisive action (Frisby 1992: 12–13). Kracauer's contemporaries, Bertold Brecht and Walter Benjamin also saw the detective novel as a distinctively modernist literary form, but found more to recommend. Both were avid fans of the genre, wrote essays during the 1930s to better understand the appeal of detective fiction, and even started work on a co-authored detective series (Herzog 2009: 14). The *Convolutes* section of Walter Benjamin's *Arcades Project*, his compendious collage of insights about the social conditions of modernity, is littered with references to Edgar Allen Poe, the originator of North American detective fiction.

All of this makes the current lack of sociological interest in detective fiction all the more striking. Within this, two recent texts stand out. The first is Todd Herzog's (2009) *Crime Stories: Criminalistic Fantasy and the Culture of Crisis in Weimar Germany*, which considers detective fiction as emblematic of the cultural crisis of Germany's inter-war years. The second is Luc Boltanski's (2014) *Mysteries and Conspiracies: Detective Stories, Spy Novels and the Making of Modern Societies*. Here, Boltanski argues that nineteenth and twentieth century detective novels participated in a historical shift wherein the nation-state's claim to offer the authoritative account of 'reality' came to be challenged and power came to be viewed with suspicion.

This book contributes to this small—but, we hope, growing—body of sociological work. It does so by offering the first in-depth sociological account of post-1970s detective fiction. We take this body of fiction to reveal important, but so far unidentified theoretical ideas about what it means to be an individual in the twenty-first century. We make a case for this in the concluding chapter. By way of introduction, and to clarify our approach: we see detective fiction as a form of sociological enquiry, able to shed light on the relationship between the individual and society, and particularly the strains of everyday life. In this, too, the book is distinct from previous sociological accounts of fiction, which generally understand its value in terms of how it can illustrate, enlarge, or help articulate a social theory.

Notes

1. Thomas de Quincey, *On Murder Considered as One of the Fine Arts; Being an Address Made to a Gentleman's Club Concerning its Aesthetic Appreciation* (first published in 1827; London, Penguin, 2015).
2. Anthony Horowitz, *The Word is Murder* (London, Century, 2017), p. 61.
3. The central character of the Akunin novels is a detective named Erast Fandorin; see, for example, *The Winter Queen* (London, Weidenfeld and Nicolson, 2003) and *Special Assignments* (London, Weidenfeld and Nicolson, 2007). Novels set in Nazi Germany include those by Philip Kerr; three were published collectively as *Berlin Noir* in 1993 by Penguin. Murder in sixteenth century England has been recorded by C.J. Sansom in the Matthew Shardlake series, the first of which is *Dissolution* (London, Macmillan, 2003). Gladys Mitchell published 66 novels featuring the detective Mrs Bradley in the period 1929 and 1984. During this period, she wrote two parodies of Agatha Christie, *The Mystery of the Butcher's Shop* (London, Gollancz, 1929) and *The Saltmarsh Murders* (London, Gollancz, 1932).
4. The first detective novel to feature a woman detective was *The Female Detective* by Andrew Forrester, first published in 1864 (London, The British Library, 2015). More recently, the central women detectives created by Sue Grafton and Sara Paretsky in the USA are, respectively, Kinsey Malone and V. I. Warshawski. Grafton's novels are set in California, those of Paretsky in Chicago. Both women, while far from trigger happy, have killed various characters.
5. The British author Nicola Upson has written a series of novels bringing back to life a real-life author (Josephine Tey) as a fictional amateur detective. The first of a series of these novels, all of which evoke the time of the 'Golden Age' of detective fiction is *An Expert in Murder* (London, Faber and Faber, 2008). In a similar homage to the work of distinguished women writers of crime fiction Stella Duffy has recently completed an unfinished novel by the distinguished writer of detective fiction Ngaio Marsh. Marsh, like Christie was a prolific author (she wrote 32 novels featuring 'her' detective Roderick Alleyn but left unfinished a final Alleyn mystery, now published as *Money in the Morgue: The New Inspector Alleyn Novel* [London, Collins Crime Club, 2018]).

6. James Foreman, *Locking Up Our Own: Crime and Punishment in Black America* (New York, Farrar, Straus and Giroux, 2017).

7. For a concise account of neo-liberalism see David Harvey, *A Brief History of Neo-liberalism* (Oxford, Oxford University Press, 2005). A more detailed account is given by Daniel Stedman-Jones in *Masters of the Universe* (Princeton, NJ, Princeton University Press, 2012).

8. The National Deviance Conference met regularly at the University of York from 1967–1975 and was hugely influential in changing many aspects of crime and policing. The Conference was revived from 2011, again at the University of York.

9. Amongst the most influential of the books about the 'new' criminology were: *The New Criminology: For a Social Theory of Deviance* (London, Routledge, 1973) by Ian Taylor, Paul Walton and Jock Young and Steve Box's *Deviance, Reality and Society* (New York, Holt, Rinehart and Winston, 1971).

10. The authors Tana French and John Harvey are notably extensive in not just the numbers but the range of their thanks.

11. Stephen Fulcher, *Catching a Serial Killer: My Hunt for the Murderer Christopher Halliwell* (London, Ebury Press, 2017).

12. DNA stands for Deoxyribonucleic Acid; HOLMES for Home Office Large Major Enquiry System; IPCC for Independent Police Crimes Commission; MIR for Major Incident Room; PACE for Police and Criminal Evidence Act; PCMH for Plea and Case Management Hearing; POLSA for Police Search Advisor; SCAS for Serious Case Analysis Section; TIE for Trace, Interrogate, Eliminate; TRL for Technology Readiness Level; VODS for Vehicle Online Descriptive Search.

13. Maj Sjöwall and Per Wahlöö, *The Man on the Balcony* (London, Harper Perennial, 2007), p. 150.

14. Stephen Fulcher, *Catching a Serial Killer*, p. 383.

15. Gary T. Marx, *Windows into the Soul: Surveillance and Society in an Age of Technology* (Chicago, Chicago University Press, 2016).

16. As well as the Macpherson judgement the case of Stephen Lawrence had far reaching implications and recognition. It resulted in the passing of the Criminal Justice Act of 2003, which rescinded the 'double jeopardy' law. In detective fiction the case re-appears in the novel by Deborah Crombie, *The Garden of Lamentations* (New York, HarperCollins, 2017) where it becomes a dream of the 'bad' past.

17. The definitive account of the Hillsborough disaster, and the aftermath, is Phil Scraton's *Hillsborough: The Truth* (Edinburgh, Mainstream Publishing, 2009). Over the course of 28 years families of the deceased fought for a change from the original coroner's court judgement of accidental death. Their campaign succeeded in 2017; the verdict was changed to 'unlawful killing due to gross negligence'.

18. For fiction on this subject see, for example, the novels of Donna Leon, set in Venice and those by Michael Dibdin, set in various parts of Italy. Scandinavian fiction is replete with examples of corruption in many state institutions; the most famous recent examples to be found in Steig Larsson's *Millennium Trilogy*. For a discussion of instances and relative levels of state and institutional corruption see B. Rothstein, 2011. The Quality of Government Corruption, Social Trust and Inequality in International Perspective (Chicago: University of Chicago Press).

19. The disabled man, Bijan Ebrahami, had repeatedly asked his local police force for protection. None was given and in 2013 Ebrahami was murdered by his neighbour, Lee James, who suspected him of being a paedophile. In February 2016 two policemen were given prison sentences for 'misconduct in a public office'.

20. Two studies, across almost thirty years, demonstrate the continuity of protest on this issue. See: Frank Parkin, *Middle Class Radicalism* (Manchester, Manchester University Press, 1968) and Sasha Roseneil, *Disarming Patriarchy: Feminism and Political Action at Greenham Common* (Buckingham, Open University Press, 1995).

21. Jonathan Powell, *Talking to Terrorists: How to End Armed Conflicts* (London, Bodley Head, 2014).

22. The research organisation INQUEST has estimated that since 1990 there have been 1990 deaths in police custody in England and Wales.

23. See Ben Crewe, A. Liebling, D. Padfield, and G. Virgo, 'Joint Enterprise: The Implications of an Unfair and an Unclear Law,' *Criminal Law Review*, Issue 4, 2015, pp. 252–269.

References

Åström, B., K. Gregersdotter, and T. Horeck (eds.). 2012. *Rape in Stieg Larsson's Millennium Trilogy and Beyond: Contemporary Scandinavian and Anglophone Crime Fiction*. Basingstoke: Palgrave Macmillan. Available at:

https://www.palgrave.com/gb/book/9780230308404#aboutBook. Accessed 14 May 2018.

Beveridge, William. 1942. *Social Insurance and Allied Services*—Beveridge Report of 1942. Available at: https://www.sochealth.co.uk/national-health-service/public-health-and-wellbeing/beveridge-report/. Accessed 14 May 2018.

Boltanski, Luc. 2014. *Mysteries and Conspiracies: Detective Stories, Spy Novels and the Making of Modern Societies.* Cambridge: Polity.

Box, Steve. 1971. *Deviance, Reality and Society.* New York: Holt, Rinehart and Winston.

Deborah, Crombie. 2017. *The Garden of Lamentations.* New York: HarperCollins.

Effron, Malcah (ed.). 2013. *The Millennial Detective: Essays on Trends in Crime Fiction, Film and Television.* Jefferson, NC: McFarland.

Forrester, Andrew. 2015 (originally 1864). *The Female Detective.* London: The British Library.

Forshaw, Barry. 2012. *Death in a Cold Climate: A Guide to Scandinavian Crime Fiction.* Basingstoke: Palgrave Macmillan.

Frisby, David. 1992. Between the Spheres: Siegfried Krakauer and the Detective Novel. *Theory Culture, Society* 9 (1): 1–22.

Gregoriou, Christiana. 2007. *Deviance in Contemporary Crime Fiction.* Basingstoke: Palgrave Macmillan.

Harvey, David. 2005. *A Brief History of Neo-liberalism.* Oxford: Oxford University Press.

Herzog, Todd. 2009. *Crime Stories: Criminalistic Fantasy and the Culture of Crisis in Weimar Germany.* USA: Berghahn Books.

Horowitz, Anthony. 2017. *The Word Is Murder.* London: Century.

Marsh, Ngaio. 2018. *Money in the Morgue: The New Inspector Alleyn Novel.* London: Collins Crime Club.

Marx, Gary T. 2016. *Windows into the Soul: Surveillance and Society in an Age of Technology.* Chicago: Chicago University Press.

Mitchell, Gladys. 1929. *The Mystery of the Butcher's Shop.* London: Gollancz.

Mitchell, Gladys. 1932. *The Saltmarsh Murders.* London: Gollancz.

Peacock, S. (ed.). 2013. *Stieg Larsson's Millennium Trilogy: Interdisciplinary Approaches to Nordic Noir in Page and Screen.* Basingstoke: Palgrave Macmillan.

Peacock, Steven. 2014. *Swedish Crime Fiction: Novel, Film, Television.* Manchester: Manchester University Press.

Powell, Jonathan. 2014. *Talking to Terrorists: How to End Armed Conflicts*. London: Bodley Head.

Sansom, Christopher John. 2003. *Dissolution*. London: Macmillan.

Sjöwall, Maj, and Per Wahlöö. 2007. *The Man on the Balcony*. London: Harper Perennial.

Stedman-Jones, Daniel. 2012. *Masters of the Universe*. Princeton: Princeton University Press.

Taylor, Ian, Paul Walton, and Jock Young. 1973. *The New Criminology: For a Social Theory of Deviance*. London: Routledge.

Upson, Nicola. 2008. *An Expert in Murder*. London: Faber and Faber.

2

The Scene of the Crime

The question of 'who did it?' and 'how did this happen?' have, in the second decade of the twenty-first century come to dominate a number of global contexts: why did Hillary Clinton lose the 2016 Presidential Election in the United States, why did the United Kingdom vote for Brexit, who killed the Swedish Prime Minister Olof Palme, and will we ever know what happened to the English child Madeleine McCann? These questions, which have pre-occupied millions of people in both our everyday and professional lives are a shared form of detection, questions to be answered about the world in which we live, and about which conclusions are often held to be based on questionable information. Not least of course because comments about 'false facts' and 'fake news' have suggested that we live in a world in which the information available to us, despite being greater in quantity and more extensive in reach than at any other time in human history, is also unreliable.

It is a contention of this book that this last point is no truer now than any other time in history. Historians of the past two centuries could point to numerous occasions when the information put before the public has differed so widely from the actual reality that it has had no claim to authority. But what many forms of information now

© The Author(s) 2019
M. Evans et al., *Detecting the Social*, https://doi.org/10.1007/978-3-319-94520-0_2

distributed about the world possess are vastly extended forms of control and distribution. Without invoking the scenario promised to us by George Orwell in his novel *1984*, we have to acknowledge that there is—to put no fine points upon it—a considerable amount of nonsense, mis-information and lies in everyday forms of the global media. But what we also have to accept is that we are as active as we have ever been in the construction of information through our own exchanges with others. Let us establish here that we are not just the passive recipients of lies, damned lies and statistics but that we in our turn reproduce that information and indeed in many cases invent our own problematic versions of the truth. In short, we act like the many of the characters portrayed in detective fiction: we absorb information from others whilst at the same time constructing our own versions of what we hold to be the truth or what we wish others to accept as the truth. Deceit, of ourselves and others, is a mainstay of both social life and also of the fiction that we will discuss.

Yet the crucial question here, for detectives in fiction quite as much as those who exist in real life, is: what exactly is the truth of any given situation? Every century of recorded history is replete with examples of the way in which human beings respond to difficult situations and attempt to discover the truth. We now know that 'evil' cannot be recognised through the ability of human beings to survive various forms of tests of the body. (A view, we should remember which did not disappear with physical tests for witchcraft but persisted well into the late nineteenth century in instances such as the phrenology practised by the Italian criminologist Cesare Lombroso.)[1] We also know that when human beings feel that they cannot understand or make sense of the reality in which they find themselves they often become angry or bored or simply refuse to engage with the outside world. All these personal emotional conditions have been long known across the social sciences and the humanities; alienation, anomie, disenchantment, disempowerment and abandonment are just a few of the names given to the sense that the world has become unknowable. These sociological terms for individual feelings about the world (and the results that those feelings produce) were a central concern for sociologists. Max Weber, Georg Simmel and Emile Durkheim wrote famous studies of the links between individual emotional worlds and social actions; in the late twentieth century writers such as Lauren Berlant and Sara Ahmed have studied what has now become termed 'affect'.[2] Yet whilst we live in a world which has educated more people than ever before in its history and puts the collection and distribution of 'knowledge' as a high social priority the gap between what we personally may understand about 'our' world and what there is to be known in the world is arguably larger than ever before.

The world of the twenty-first century is not, we would argue, necessarily more self-aware about itself than it has been in the past. Yes, the sources of immediate information are greater, as is the reach of that information. But those questions about 'what is going on' or 'what caused that' are as contentious and complex as they ever were. Certainly, many of us are less inclined to look to the supernatural or the divine for explanation (and of course all religions of the book rely on the 'knowledge' of the divine for their authenticity) but human agency is often no less puzzling than that of the gods.

Into this void of incomprehension and confusion step any number of usual suspects, anxious to offer their own interpretations of contemporary events. These figures are capable—given the present reach of the global media—of acquiring immediate access to the public. Men such as Donald Trump and Nigel Farage might not always be thought of in terms of the veracity of the information that informs their various politics, but both offer what many people have found convincing in an incomprehensible world: narratives about the dangers of 'others' and the possibility of recovering fantasy visions of the past. The empirical basis of the politics of these two men is often more than slight but it is a narrative which offers a solution to a problem. The problem in the case of the politics of these two men is not a dead body, the classic starting point for detective fiction. The villains are not a single wrong-doer but collective suspects: the foreigner, the terrorist or ideas which upset certain kinds of traditional, and often xenophobic, patriarchal, values. All these generalised others come together to form a threat to the contemporary world. It is ironic that when George Orwell published his famous essay in 1946 on 'The Decline of the English Murder' he offered as an explanation for this decline the explanation of 'the new

'Americanised' world. So, two politicians are offering the public a fear of the other as the basis of their politics; precisely the collective subject of those 'new' murders which Orwell condemned.[3]

The fears manufactured and exploited by Trump and Farage stand in the long line of the manufacture of fears about 'others' which have dominated politics in much of the world for centuries. These two individuals are, as suggested, examples of those 'usual suspects' who offer their own, highly speculative explanations of social events, in which threats from 'others' are paramount. In terms of supposed threats from both outside and within societies there are similar traditions in the cultural exploration of the ideas of danger and evil. It is in this tradition (of fears of alien others, witches, evil spirits and wicked gods) that detective fiction stands. Its origins in the late eighteenth and early nineteenth centuries were similar to those of conventional fiction: the creation of a central character, grounded in, and acted in, the context of forms of recognisable reality.[4] But in early detective fiction, indeed in many contemporary instances, evil was represented by two very specific individuals: a binary in which an evil person was investigated by a good person. (If this person was not, as was the case for Sherlock Holmes, entirely 'good' in the conventional sense then at least he was 'good enough' to act as a force against evil.) This was not about the explanation of war, or plague or invasion: it was about why certain human beings felt inclined to kill or inflict various forms of violence and harm on specific others. From the first stories by William Godwin, Edgar Allen Poe and many others the public was provided with stories about the un-masking, the identification and finally the punishment of the guilty person.[5]

In the decades between the early nineteenth century and the present-day detective fiction has undergone various forms of transformation, including those changes common to other forms of fiction: more varied discussions of physical and psychological violence and sexuality, the wider geographical range and the articulation of a more complex form of the normative order. But one thing has not changed about detective fiction is its social concern and the centrality of the social world to its narrative. So—and here a generalisation is offered which covers all forms of fiction of the global north in the past one hundred years—detective fiction often offers to the reader a much greater understanding of social change and its general impact than does more conventional fiction. For instance, an engagement with the impact of the globalisation of capital or the problematic interventions of the welfare state do not occupy a place of structural significance in much of mainstream fiction. In the million seller volumes of Jo Nesbø and Stieg Larsson these issues are fundamental; they constitute in themselves the role of inanimate characters in the narrative. It is this identification of the lived experience of life in the later decades of twentieth century and the first decades of the twenty-first century that makes detective fiction so distinct in its concerns. It is also, and centrally here, the content which makes detective fiction so much an active protagonist in itself: the written embodiment of the idea of detecting the modern. Rather than provide 'background' to the lives of characters detective fiction makes the world in which millions of us live a character, albeit a non-human one, in its fiction. In doing so, what some detective fiction arguably achieves is a blurring of those conventional lines between fiction and non-fiction. To illustrate the collective consequences for individuals of state policies about overseas empires or the growth of the trade in recreational drugs—as for example the work of the English writer William Shaw or the Swedish writer Jens Lapidus does—is to explore the possibilities of that longstanding question of the inter-relationship and the inter-action between the social and the personal.[6]

This issue which detective fiction investigates is not one—as the work of Durkheim, Simmel, Freud and many others suggest—which is short of interpretation. Even if Trump and his ilk are not credible as informed students of the social world they stand at one end of a continuum of investigation which reaches from the entirely incompetent and ill-informed to the highly sophisticated. What brings the individual and collective voices together on this continuum are two shared forms of recognitions: that global capitalism is our planet's dominant form of political economy and that the world has at its command weapons that could ensure its complete destruction. After that, differences do more than merely emerge: they become the very matter of politics and political disagreement. So that, whilst agreement exists about the extensive reach of global capitalism agreement does not exist about the benefits, and the beneficiaries, of this political system. Equally, weapons of mass destruction exist as reality for everyone; the validity of their use and their continued manufacture is much more divisive. But what perhaps unites the various positions on this continuum about the contemporary world is that we all share a sense of danger: the danger of those 'others' certainly but also the other kinds of danger about, for example, an exploitation of the world's resources so comprehensive that it could endanger the lives of future generations. In short, the modern world is not, to many people, a safe world.

Quite where that safe world was, and is, remains a highly contentious question. In this the detective fiction of much of the early part of the twentieth century made assumptions about social safety, and safe communities which historical hindsight might now only find extraordinary. The village of Miss Jane Marple in the fiction of Agatha Christie was largely untroubled by the rise of fascism or the Depression. The detective fiction of the United States in the same decades, even as it had a greater engagement with the urban world, had much of the same social blindness. The problems of poverty and deprivation which were central to the varied post 1945 constructions of the welfare states seldom appear in this literature as issues of structural significance. It was not that Miss Marple's St. Mary Mead did not have its upsetting episodes and untimely deaths, but it was a place that could be restored to safety, to the reliable form of its existence. The social world could be re-constituted and re-constructed. Christie, in common with writers of English canonical fiction of the nineteenth century will even achieve this re-building through the marriage of some of her characters. Yet if we simply accept this reading of Christie and Golden Age fiction what we refuse are a number of important themes. The first is that the re-creation (in film and television) of Christie's work in the late twentieth and early twenty-first century is consistently presented through a nostalgic gaze and an implicit eulogy for a vanished past. The second point is that within many works of Golden Age fiction there is a powerful element of subversive politics. To illustrate this point, it is only necessary to turn to the constantly sceptical eye of Miss Jane Marple, directed as it often was onto the competence of the English police force. Although never directly critical of any member of the police force (despite the considerable provocation offered by this group in terms of the refusal of Miss

Marple's intelligence) she consistently challenges not just the judgments of the police but the basis of their judgments. It is unlikely that Christie wrote in order to offer an ontological challenge to the conventional world and yet this is exactly what Miss Marple is capable of doing: of speaking truth to power, as Quaker teaching has always insisted.

What can be seen in the implicit politics of Christie's work is not just a woman's criticism of institutionalised forms of masculinity (notably, in this context, the police force that allowed little access for women in the years between 1918–1939) but also a politics of regret and reproach about the masculinised and militarised forms of power which had led, in 1914–1918 to the catastrophic losses of war. Christie is not of course an explicit critic of the politics of the First World War but there are surely connections between that appalling loss of life, often conducted in forms of rigid stupidity and carelessness for human lives, with the clumsy attitudes and limited horizons of the police. The failings of the police are further repeated in that other context of often damaging and thoughtless policing, the policing of the British Empire, which is epitomised in the figure of Colonel Hastings. This sometime companion of Christie's other major creation, Hercule Poirot, is just one instance of that often repeated bringing together of two detectives: one who embodies sophisticated intelligence and maverick attitudes to the world in general, the other the representative of all that is conventional. Set against Hercule Poirot, who is ever mindful of many of the limitations as well as the strengths of the British, we meet in Hastings a man who has brought home with him from the British Empire an essential simplicity in his view of the world. (We first meet Poirot as both a victim of British foreign policy but also someone allowed access to a safe refuge).[7] Again, the contrast that Christie points us to if we read beyond the commemoration of a mythical past, is to different ways of understanding the world and the dangers of assuming moral and social homogeneity. In the 1920s and 1930s emergent forms of modernity were not universally accepting of the conventions which have been retrospectively imposed upon it.

It is therefore possible to suggest that Miss Jane Marple is a precursor, in detective fiction, of much of what Virginia Woolf was to say in 1938 in *Three Guineas* and that other feminists were saying throughout the inter-war period.[8] Woolf's book is a furious onslaught on all forms of male authority and it emerged from those same social circumstances as that of Christie and Miss Marple. These connections, between two great and prolific women writers are important, because what they suggest is that it is possible to see in detective fiction more than simply a pursuit of a guilty party. Much more—as Christie knew—was at stake in this process, not least the arrest and punishment of a person through whom moral certainty might be re-established. But both women knew that behind the elaborate manners and behaviour of high culture, lay alliances of gendered power and determined forms of exclusion. Moreover, as both women also recognised those patterns did not work for everyone; in different ways Woolf and Christie, together with other feminist voices of the inter-war years, protested against the exclusion and the marginalisation of women from various institutions and locations of power and privilege, not least that of the power of personal autonomy. Some of these absolute certainties about both gender and class that had been maintained up to 1939 were swept away when war broke out. The exigences that followed differed widely between the combatants: Nazi Germany maintained, for example, traditional expectations about the employment of married women and instigated pro-natalist policies about parenthood.[9] Britain, and to a lesser extent the United States, took steps not just to encourage the employment of women but to enforce it. The 'People's War' as the historian Angus Calder has described the conduct of the war in Britain brought with it both the inevitable mobilisation of the armed services but also the civilian population and enforced regulations which emphasised social solidarity, a solidarity which could not be maintained alongside existing hierarchies.[10] Some of the radical measures made necessary through the demands of war were not maintained after 1945 and as Calder and other historians of the Second World War have pointed out, the extent of social transformation did not add up to the still perpetuated myth of 'all in this together'.[11] Nevertheless, the social as well as the material impact of the war brought with it a need for radical forms of reconstruction. Thus, much of the global north after 1945 brought in measures that generalised the expectation that all citizens have the right to vote and social protection from want and ill health.

But many of the social divisions remained. Detective fiction, in common with conventional fiction, began to identify problematic cracks in what was supposed to be—and was presented as such—a new era of prosperity and peace. Christie was no exception to this shift: in her novel *The Mirror Crack'd from Side to Side* (first published in 1962 but set in 1953) she identified the costs to individuals of a consumer culture and the encroachment of the suburbs on rural life. In placing the events of her novel in the past she provided a sense of the experience of those changes for the people living through them. That same fictional device, of situating novels in a recent past, has continued in detective fiction to the present. William Shaw's Tozer and Breen novels are set at the beginning of the 1960s: a decade of conflict and change throughout the west.[12] The legacies of conflicts in overseas colonies gave rise to new forms and locations of armed conflict, the wealth accrued through a greater emphasis on consumer consumption did not bring with it significant increases in social mobility or access to power; traditional elites did not disappear, rather they changed aspects of their cultural identity. As the rate of technological change became evident in the goods available for everyday consumption as much as in military consumption the 'modern' became, in material terms, a reality. But it did not, as more and more people began to realise, bring about a world of social equality; ancient divisions of class, race and gender remained. The idea of the 'modern' despite the goods and the services that it brought with it became, by 1970, not just tarnished, but also a place in which the threat of danger was taking different forms. The populations of the global north were no longer vulnerable to famine or plague, but they were vulnerable to various forms of loss and danger: the perceived loss of communities, the distance between individuals and sites of power, the diseases and insecurities of affluence and the increasing pollution of the environment.

This was not what the modern world had been supposed to achieve, or the situation of the individual within it. We had been led to believe that as we became better educated, able to live longer and had more healthy lives, we would be more, rather than less able, to exercise those 'choices' which were the favoured mantra and mainstay of politicians. New forms of the legitimacy of personal choices—specifically in sexual identity—allowed more people, in some countries, a central form of control over definitions and experiences of intimacy but exercising this form of choice was not, it was increasingly apparent, accompanied by greater shared prosperity or security. As the historian Selina Todd has written in her history of Great Britain in the twentieth century:

> ...1979 was a watershed when, for the first time in forty years, the gap between the richest and the poorest began to widen rapidly, and Britain witnessed the fall of the working class as an economic and political force.[13]

This gap has not decreased. By the beginning of the twenty-first century new perceptions of the lives of millions of people has emerged: the 'precariat' had become an acknowledged term about the lack of job security and income of significant sections of the population. The term the 'squeezed middle' became another label used to describe the circumstances of a part of the population which had once been supposed to live in relative security. Rates of social inequality attracted political attention at the same time as social scientists, by the beginning of the second decade of the twenty-first century had begun to speak of the chasms emerging in both wealth and income between the many and the few.[14]

In this context, both fiction and non-fiction began to re-assess expectations about the world of the twenty-first century. Amongst those writing non-fiction, there emerged a broad consensus that increasing forms of social inequality were not only morally unacceptable—as many had always supposed them to be—but also the source of social breakdown and cohesion. Despite the persistence of neo-liberal ideas, particularly that of the value of limiting the extent of state supported services, voices from across the political spectrum began to regard aspects of the life of the late twentieth century as deeply problematic. On the left of the political spectrum writers such as Luc Boltanski suggested that Marxists had to think about 'new' forms of capitalism in which cultural change began to be far more significant than material and economic change; as such an increasingly powerful driver of the direction of politics.[15] The new changes in various forms of gender relationships demonstrated that previous certainties about the ways in which groups and other forms of social association are made has to be re-thought; an issue arousing both deeply hostile and energetically enthusiastic views. In this, what both sides of the debate could see was that the normative hold that communities, neighbourhoods and conventional expectations of the family once had begun to decrease, whilst the attraction and the promise of more diverse forms of the self-increased. For all parties in these debates what was equally apparent was the appeal of what has become known as 'celebrity culture', a global form of both real and imagined existence that increasingly took over from those perceptions and constructs of existence formed in, and by, more local contexts. Our imagination about ourselves began to exist more firmly in the abstract and the distant rather than in the immediate. This is not to say that fantasies about ourselves have not always existed. What is different and what is being suggested as a profoundly important aspect of the modern here is that there is more social space for those fantasies, because fantasies have become central to the market's ongoing search for new markets and new sources of profit. But, and it is a hugely important but, those fantasies, as much as they might be achieved are also being sought in circumstances of much increased insecurity of all kinds. Hence the paradox of the modern; a world rich in vastly diverse forms of both material and cultural production and consumption but increasingly experienced and lived through circumstances of material insecurity. In the detective fiction of the world since 1970 this 'precarity' of existence has become fundamental to the circumstances in which characters live out their lives. A final word on this topic: to point out that the dissolution of social bonds in the twentieth century was predicted long before 1970. In 1912 E. J. Urwick wrote in his *A Philosophy of Social Progress* that:

> In our modern life the sense of unity is not realized, and all the pervading duties of citizenship are lost sight of in the wilderness of both individuals and groups.[16]

This quotation demonstrates that questions about social cohesion, or its lack of, have long been discussed and debated across the social sciences, with much of that work expressing considerable pessimism about the future. In non-fiction, and specifically in detective fiction, the lived experience of the more perilous world of the present has become ever more central. This is not to say that the world in which Christie, Hammett and Chandler wrote did not have its own insecurities; although the major traumas of the twentieth century—centrally the Second World War—seldom figure in the plots of the fiction. So here we can start to detect a central characteristic which marks off detective fiction of the world before 1970 with the decades that follow: before 1970 the circumstances which matter in detective fiction are generally those of the local and the particular. After 1970 detective fiction goes global: the world of the decade after the oil crisis and the coming to power of the ideology of neo-liberalism and the politics of Thatcher and Reagan is a world which becomes central to the plots of detective fiction. In short, writers of detective fiction increasingly recognised the worlds outside their own countries and localities.

So, in detecting this new characteristic of detective fiction a few references to the 'clues' about its manifestation are essential: to ask not just how it happened but what kinds of differences to the detective novel were brought with it. A central, unmissable, 'clue' is that characters start to live in more widely and easily connected worlds. It is not therefore that a character in a Jo Nesbø or Stieg Larsson novel might, literally, travel the world but also that the events of the world as much as the local impinge upon and construct the motives and the actions of the characters. In Christie's St. Mary Mead or Colin Dexter's Morse novels set in Oxford it is essentially local rivalries or jealousies that form the plot. For example, one of the Morse novels centres upon competition for the mastership for an Oxford College. It is an instance of possible achievement that might matter to very few people (or indeed have implications for even fewer people) and is a very local event. The comment 'who cares?' might well be made about both the form of competition here and the events surrounding it: deeply unattractive, over-privileged and over-educated people competing for something that is at the very best of minority interest. Outside the life of this particular Oxford College few people would have much invested in the outcome of this power struggle.

But in Larsson and Nesbø in Scandinavia or Matthew Frank in England or Ian Rankin in Scotland the actions that take place on the page have a more general resonance. It actually matters to considerable numbers of people that the social services are corrupt, that polluted and illegal drugs are being distributed on a large scale, that housing projects are constructed by incompetent firms. All these authors—and many others—fall into the general category of *noir*, that is to say a coherent and consistent vision of the darkness at the heart of the modern. Of course, the word itself associates, in ways which have come implications for racial politics, the colour black with evil or bad things. But we might also see in criticisms of this term when used about the many writers termed 'noir' something of what psychoanalysis would name as 'denial', the public refusal to recognise or come to terms with those things which it finds difficult to countenance. Certainly, 'noir' fiction does not invest in happy endings: there are very few positive endings and if anything, the overwhelming sense of the ending is that of loss, disappointment and the unresolved.

What is central to much of detective fiction post 1970 is that it changed because of its collective recognition of a changed and changing world. For the origin of this shift we should note that by 1970 both technology and economic theory had begun to be global. 'World 'wars had dominated the politics of much of the twentieth century but what became increasingly apparent was the inter-dependence of economies across the planet. For example, by the end of the 1970s it had become more than obvious to anyone living in a country dependent upon fossil fuel for its continued existence that the world was indeed a connected place. At the same time the benefits of the 'modern' which populations of the global north had begun to assume as an essential part of daily life were not necessarily reliable and predictable but depended on new forms of fragile and uncertain political alliances. When the UK government of Edward Heath brought in the 'Three Day' week in 1974 and citizens were exhorted to 'clean their teeth in the dark' it became clear that certainties about the optimistic confidence of the continuation of the western way of life were unfounded. Central to this uncertainty was the growing determination of many countries in the global south that their resources and their needs should not be regarded as of secondary importance to those of the global north. This new form of political engagement is central to detective fiction after 1970: sometimes described as 'post colonialism' it is widely located in writers of noir.

In various ways certainty about the modern began to flounder. It was an uncertainty that affected many forms of political and intellectual life but in this particular context of detective fiction post 1970 there are a number of specific changes. First, it becomes evident that the 'enclosed plot' is no longer of interest. That most famous form of detective story—the 'locked room' mystery—vanishes from the genre even though confinement reappears in those plots where unfortunate individuals are kept prisoner in underground spaces. But more generally, the location of the plot, the village or the streets where the evil deeds take place becomes an enlarged space. There is, quite simply, in fiction as in reality, a world outside the local. But more than that what emerges in 'noir' fiction is that the literal physical space of the locked room has been replaced by the ability of both heroes and villains to navigate virtual space. The *Millennium Trilogy's* Lisbeth Salander can make (and break) lives from the keyboard of her lap top. In the same trilogy, the computer genius, known by the name of Plague, who supports Salander in her on line world, lives in one squalid room. This new form of a locked room is a place from which external events (good and bad) are controlled. A reversal of a more traditional fictional form in which the bad events happened in the closed space. The general loss of that closed space is perhaps the reason why some detective writers insist on retaining plots which involve the imprisonment of victims in small spaces.[17] In both cases what is occurring is an examination of the limits of literal, physical space. It is no novelty in fiction that fictional characters have railed against what they see as the limits of their world. It is the cry of Charlotte Bronte's Jane Eyre for 'more of practical experience than I possessed' or the fantasies of Flaubert's Madame Bovary about the lives of the rich. The difference however is that the wider world of the twenty-first century has become a more active and more invasive protagonist in everyday lives. We are encouraged to want and to desire in ways that are profitable for others; if we become harmed by this culture we are unknown, random victims. That link—which once was so straightforward between various forms of wanting and getting—has become more complex, distant and more liable to highly dubious forms of manipulation.[18]

With this, of course, the existence of every human being on the planet has changed and changed in two ways in particular which are central to post 1970s crime fiction. The first is the growing diversity of the social space in which this fiction occurs. Whilst some writers—for example Nesbø or Jens Lapidus paint a broad geographical canvas—others such as Karin Fossum or Ragnar Jónasson—continue to choose those small, isolated communities as the locations of their fiction. Locations which are more reminiscent of previous generations of crime writing. Yet what unites these contexts is the need for detection to reveal what is hidden, for detectives to force communities, be they large or small scale to recognise the extent, both geographical and historical, of the abuses and the cruelties that they have been refusing. But what we have to see in fictional detection is that it articulates the continued need to admit the inequities and injustices of the past that has inspired those real-life campaigns for 'revelation' that have long been a part of British life for the past decades. If we look back at what we can describe as campaigns for recognition and against concealment—for example about the effects of Thalidomide, the negative effects of traffic fumes or the abuse and 'grooming' of teenage girls in northern cities of the UK—we see that campaigners, be they private individuals or more organised groups, have had to struggle for years to achieve any kind of admission of responsibility by the guilty or recompense for the victims. What is also notable, and this is particularly true of the many campaigns fought (and still being fought) about various contexts of the abuse of children is that many public institutions have been involved but are often slow to act or to assume responsibility. A recent BBC documentary about what has become known as the Rochdale Abuse Scandal demonstrated that the police, social workers and schools had all been aware of the grooming of young women from about 2005 yet it was not until almost ten years later that prosecutions were brought, resulting in the conviction and the imprisonment of those guilty.[19] The length of time between the actual acts of abuse and cruelty is, as the novels of, for example, William Shaw, Val McDermid and Yrsa Sigurðardóttir make clear, often considerable.[20]

This distance between knowledge, or suspicion, of criminal and abusive behaviour and intervention about it, is not of course a unique characteristic of the twenty-first century. But the issue that it raises here are the implications of this distance in the twenty-first century between the length of time in reality for the exposure of abusive acts and the fictional accounts which assume the ease of the recognition of 'evil'. Here there is perhaps a dramatic difference between detective fiction on the two sides of the Atlantic and the way in which these differences contribute to different forms of politics. For example, we might suggest that the fiction of Patricia Cornwell, replete with references to guns and sophisticated technology, encourages and supports the view that 'evil' can be rapidly countered and eliminated. It is a view which is entirely collusive with those politics which assume that rapid militarised campaigns will immediately produce a resolution. What is also maintained here is the view that the motives for criminal acts are essentially individual in their origins. Not that Cornwell does not present detailed information about the pathology of individuals—that is meticulously set out—but what is perhaps missing is a sense of the connections between that pathology and general and collective forms of social life. It is all too easy to suppose that there is no such thing as society, let alone social impact, in these novels. Cornwell is an example, albeit a sophisticated and very successful one, of the 'find and shoot' crime fiction that finds its most natural home in the United States, a country which almost uniquely in the global north allows its citizens an almost unfettered access to guns. An access which is legitimated by powerful lobbies and significant sections of the population.

Outside the United States, where the legitimacy of civilian access to guns is less general and less endorsed we nevertheless find that those in pursuit of criminals are also often armed. Europe is not a gun free zone. Jo Nesbø's Harry Hole often carries a gun, sometimes legitimately, sometimes less so. But what Nesbø makes of this, in common with other European writers, is that the gun is the last resort, and to be used as much in defence of the detective as in the elimination of the criminal. So, what we have, in much of European detective fiction, is a view that is not only less supportive of armed detectives but also gives less credence to the idea that gunning down 'evil' people may be an effective way to secure public safety. The implication of this is that we can consider a radical disjunction between those societies and public cultures which sanction the view that the response to individual 'evil' can be what is described in the Cornwell novels as the 'elimination of the perp' and those which at least in part consider that criminal and abusive behaviour as more complex in its origin. This difference is important because it allows us to recognise that detective fiction is anything but homogeneous in its moral universe. At a point where detective fiction is becoming more 'global' in the reach and context of its plots this is a central recognition to maintain. It is too easy, and of course a part of those politics which have given rise to fierce resistance to the west, to assume that the norms and aspirations of the west are the aspirations of the entire planet. For many of us who live in the west it is as important for differences within the west to be acknowledged.

How this relates to the issue of the recognition of crime and criminal behaviour is that in what can be described as the immediate armed response model, coupled with assumptions of a homogeneous global morality, there is very little suggestion of two aspects of the social world: that criminal behaviour emerges from a mix of the social and the individual and that the struggle against it involves often complex forms of recognition. Which is why, perhaps, detective fiction outside the United States often depends upon the discovery of a long distant crime: what is being tacitly acknowledged here is exactly that failure of social infrastructure to act and identify crime as was the case in those instances cited above. What we are confronting in this are diverse views of our collective experience: views which on the one hand assume that crime only exists in the present and those which consider the ways in which the present is formed by the recognition of what has not been acknowledged or confronted. The very different attitudes to the detection, the perpetration and the confrontation of crime both involve different politics. One, of course, recalls a national past as 'great', the other is more accepting of the idea of the constant, trans historical, possibility of shifting patterns of moral and civic virtue. In this difference what we see is a confrontation between accounts of the world which assume a moral certainty about the values of a market economy, a naturalisation of the values of entrepreneurship and private property, and on the other hand, more diffuse ideas about the form of moral certainty. This latter theme is apparent in the radical, and avowedly Marxist, critique of the capitalist state evident in the Swedish police procedural novels of Sjöwall and Wahlöö.[21] In this series of novels, written in the 1960s and generally hailed as the defining precursors of post 1970s 'noir', the central character, Martin Beck, is consistently an agent of the state and yet far from sympathetic to it.

What is opening up here, and will be further explored in Chapter 3, is the suggestion that moral responsibility for criminal and murderous acts lies not just with the perpetrator but with institutions and with those others who might regard themselves, or be regarded, as innocent. What is being asked is the question of why people behave in the ways that they do, including those instances when agency takes a violent and murderous form. In many ways this question—although not necessarily a question which is framed in the context of detective fiction—is a central issue of the European Enlightenment because that set of collective ideas began to examine aspects of religious authority, not least the concept of the Devil, the Satan of literature and theology. In that examination and challenge it was inevitable that the question should be asked of why the roving eye of the Devil should fasten upon particular people. It was accepted that sin, and sinning, was a possibility but that still left the issue of why it is that people united by every apparent similarity should come to be so different in their behaviour. The question also provides a link to those who have written that the rise of detective fiction occurs because of the loss, in the west, of God and religious observance.[22] The belief in the literal embodiment of 'evil' in human beings, so much a forceful assumption in the persecution of witches and other folk devils, did not engage with the question how evil came to inhabit or control a specific individual. The Devil, in some shape or form, came to direct human actions. The idea of the controlling 'devil' provided enough explanation for the existence of evil. 'Evil', when detected, took a physical form that could be tested in various brutal ways or could be banished through forms of exorcism. The growth of the 'rational' as a normative concept—or at least the growing belief in its authority—diminished public acceptance of the idea that a body could be tested for its 'evil' qualities. As studies of the decline in witchcraft all show persecutions for witchcraft declined in the west from the seventeenth century onwards, entirely congruent with the emergence of the central themes of an 'enlightened' Europe.[23] As belief in the forms and the practice of magic disappeared, followed by the weakening of the ties of religious observance, new constructions of the idea of evil began to take their place. In terms of the links between growing secularisation and the development of detective fiction it might also be suggested that what was no longer recognised as 'revelation' through the teachings of Christianity now became revelation in the unmasking of the criminal.

These readings of history and the rise of the genre of detective fiction in the early nineteenth century implicitly suggest that societies cannot exist without forms of moral demonisation and exclusion; by association that human beings cannot exist without, if not moral binaries then at least moral certainties. But this account also raises questions about the idea of the triumph of the European Enlightenment. From the late 1930s onwards, critics such as Theodor Adorno and Max Horkheimer began to raise questions about the certainty of the validation of 'reason'.[24] After the events of the Second World War it became apparent that 'reason' was not necessarily on the side of what most people would consider virtue.

But what this left for those who wrote fiction in the second half of the twentieth century was how to write about 'evil'. In one sense it was solved through the acknowledgment of the moral legitimacy of Allied institutions in the years after 1945. The societies that defeated Hitler could be assumed to have morally capable and irreproachable institutions. In the 1950s on both sides of the Atlantic there emerged the good, intelligent, policeman: Ed McBain 'saved' the police force of the United States from previous judgments about its incompetence and corruption.[25] In Europe 'good' and professionally employed policemen gradually began to appear in all forms of the media, so that by 1970 these (largely) male, white, figures such as P.D. James's Adam Dalgleish and Ruth Rendell's Chief Inspector Wexford had replaced the talented amateurs of Christie and Sayers in Britain or the private detectives in Hammett and Chandler.

Yet these excellent gentlemen did not differ, in one crucial way, from their predecessors: they pursued single individuals, motivated by three dominant themes: jealousy, greed and shame. In all these instances what is important is that the driving motive (jealousy and others) derives from individual circumstances rather than a complex mix of the social and the individual. Such straightforward motives are as ancient and trans-cultural as the jealousies between Cain and Abel. These accounts afford the individual much the same status as any of the 'evil' people pursued and persecuted in any earlier century 'since what is also in place is a moral binary: the villains and/or murderers are clearly bad, their pursuers equally transparently good. That form of moral certainty has been the wish of countless regimes and is rarely achieved. Not the least of the spoils of victory for the Allied cause in 1945 was the re-legitimization and the re-energising of its institutions. This was accomplished not only because of military victory but because of the new forms of civic and material rights which were put in place for many of the citizens of Europe after 1945.

The post war vision of societies offering all citizens lives free of economic hardship was one that remained a central and largely consensual part of the politics of much of Europe until the beginning of the 1970s, when the focus of political energy came to be concentrated around rather different issues than those which had pre-occupied politicians in the immediate post-war years. One was various issues around the intimate and personal life of citizens (the politics of sexuality and legal arrangements about marriage) whilst the other was the increasing discussion about who and how far individuals should be supported by the state. The question was framed in terms of the imagined possibilities of the abuse of state support, even though reliable evidence for this was negligible. It was not as if this was a new issue, and certainly not in Britain. As Selina Todd has pointed out, from the early decades of the twentieth century there has been a consistent argument about how much state support should be given to individuals. Writing about the implementation of the British benefits system in the 1930s she remarks that:

> The architects of the benefits system, and those who policed it, insisted on behaving as though personal fecklessness caused poverty, and called on the unemployed to help themselves.[26]

These themes have continued to the present day, albeit in different forms. But one consistent connection that is made is that between the need of a society to 'modernise' and to 'progress'. Judgements about welfare provision in the 1930s, quite as much as in the second decade of the twenty-first century have been voiced through invocations of this kind.

The constant engagement with this narrative of being and remaining 'modern' is one that has had a consistent place in the politics of the UK since the early nineteenth century and the pursuit of and challenge to this idea has endlessly been played out in fiction as well as political reality. When, in Jane Austen's novel *Mansfield Park*, the wealthy Sir Thomas Bertram upbraided his penniless niece Fanny Price for her refusal of a highly acceptable marriage proposal, he accused her of being 'modern'. By which he meant that women should not follow the suspect 'modern' idea of thinking and choosing for themselves. Unfortunately for Sir Thomas many women (including Fanny Price) did precisely that and by 1970, as had been common throughout the nineteenth and twentieth century, many were continuing to follow Fanny's example. In 1970 we meet a coming together of numerous forms of dis-satisfaction with the authority of the narratives which had supported much of Europe throughout the immediate post war years. Fiction and film had recognised much of this dissatisfaction. Shelagh Delaney's play *A Taste of Honey*, for example, had brought together themes of the politics of class, race and gender in 1956 and films such as *The Loneliness of the Long-Distance Runner* and *Saturday Night and Sunday Morning* had shown a different view of the formal complacency of 1950s Britain. Yet it appeared to many—and certainly the British Labour Party—that what was needed was more modernisation, the 'white hot heat of the technological revolution' which the Labour leader Harold Wilson promised in 1963.

For a time, this modernising project took forward various forms of social transformation. But as the essentially national politics of the time came to meet more international challenges, it started to become clear that these changes and a continuation of the expectation of full employment and personal affluence could only be maintained through access to raw materials—crucially energy—which was no longer being granted on terms so positive to the UK. The economy of the UK had always been global but now new kinds of negotiation were emerging, forms of negotiation in which old certainties and expectations about rights to power were being transformed.

These emergent differences were hopeful to some, challenging to others. To all they raised the perennial question of how we are to live together, and it is here that detective fiction from the 1970s onwards has concerned itself with questions that concern us all. The first of these questions was, as ever, the issue of what constitutes morality; the second and the concern here is the closely related question of how we are to define ourselves, what should be the foundation and origin of our values and how we should fill our internal psychic space. Whereas once this question was answered for many people by religious belief and the various moralities sustained by it the extensive departure from formal religious observance has opened up new possibilities. Amongst the most powerful beliefs of much of the west in the twenty-first century is the view that mentally 'healthy' and stable people live in—or aspire to—stable relationships with other human beings. As detective fiction has been energetic in proposing, particularly since 1970, this is very much easier said than done. Further, this aspiration to the collective state has been consistently maintained and very much endorsed by the example of our continuation of the ancient suspicion of those living alone. That state was always assumed to be that of the female witch or a male figure of evil. In Mary Shelley's *Frankenstein*, the Creature (the being brought into existence through science) becomes dangerous because he cannot create for himself social or intimate relations. This Creature (brought to fictional life by Shelley in 1818) has become the template for a thousand reproductions of the lonely, inherently dangerous figure. Little wonder that those famous highly intelligent, intuitive detectives—from Holmes to Hole—are seldom allowed to live entirely alone.

So, we continue to demonstrate our fears of the 'loner'. We have become energetic, certainly in Britain, in the view that 'loners' are odd, if not actually dangerous. The unfortunate Bristol man Christopher Jefferies, falsely accused of murder, was arrested largely on the basis of what was interpreted as a suspicious and solitary way of life.

Christopher Jefferies was eventually entirely vindicated and able to claim considerable damages from the police. But in a similar way the killer of the British MP Jo Cox, Thomas Mair, was first described by the police as a 'loner', a view rapidly contradicted by his neighbours and those who had known him as a kind and helpful member of the community. These real-life examples about the ways in which stereotypes about the 'loner' are part of the narrative of real crime have been articulated for decades in crime fiction. Yet one of the most persistent characteristics of much of crime fiction is that the detective is also—if not a loner—then at least a person who has considerable difficulties in relating to others. From Sherlock Holmes to Inspector Morse and Harry Hole many detectives have considerable difficulty in relating to others and maintaining stable relations with others. It is not that many of these individuals do not wish to have close relationships with others but that their determination to pursue suspects finds them constantly at war with the usual conditions of intimacy with others. Hence many detectives (contemporary and otherwise) wish for, if not domestic then at least intimate life, and are as deeply suspicious of much of the public of 'the loner'.

The evidence of this consistent tradition suggests that we continue to be as deeply suspicious about the person living alone as in those previous centuries when elderly, single women were defined as problematic if not actually witches. At the same time, we also recognise, in the twenty-first century the toxic possibilities of living with others: the various forms of violence, the constraint and the exploitation. But in this lies a complexity: the very state of which we are suspicious—being an adult living alone—is also the condition of autonomy and individualism which we are increasingly encouraged to embrace. The many tensions surrounding this contradiction are part and parcel of what has informed much of the most socially informed and sensitive detective fiction of the twenty-first century. Those tensions have not become less in the twenty-first century but have—again as detective fiction has recognised—become more powerful. Absence from the home and unreliable participation in the domestic world are not, for many people, choices but the inevitable consequence of the increasing precarity of various forms of paid work and the disappearance of various forms of state supported services that once supported aspects of domestic life. In the context of these rapid changes it is instructive to compare works of detective fiction from Scandinavia, which suggest the transformations occurring in both social and psychic relations in the twenty-first century, with Ian Rankin's *Let it Bleed*, first published in 1995. All these books are published at different points in the transformation of the countries of the global north towards the ever greater social inequality which occurred in the period between 1980 and 2008. To begin with those from Scandinavia: the first is Henning Mankell's *The White Lioness*, written in 1993 and the second the *Stockholm Trilogy* by Jens Lapidus, written between 2008 and 2015. *The White Lioness* tells of a plot to assassinate Nelson Mandela and the way in which that intersects with the quiet town of Mankell's detective, Kurt Wallender. The three volumes of The *Stockholm Trilogy* follow the lives of two characters living in Stockholm, the Swede Johan Westland and the immigrant from Columbia, Jorge Salinas Barrio.

Although these novels are both set in the same country, within a close time frame, the differences in terms of events, aspirations, policing and the meaning of the law say a great deal about both the speed and the nature of social change in the late twentieth and early twenty-first centuries. Here, for example, is Kurt Wallender considering his reaction to what appears to be an inexplicable and entirely random death:

> Where do I go from here? He said to himself. I don't want anything to do with ruthless killers, with no respect for life. I don't want to get involved in a kind of violence that will be incomprehensible to me as long as I live. Maybe the next generation of policemen in this country will have a different kind of experience and have a different view of their work. But it's too late for me. I'll never be any different from what I am, a pretty good policeman in a medium-sized Swedish police district.[27]

In the event Wallender does get involved in considerable violence, but the body count is slim when compared to the kind of carnage that is unleashed in the *Stockholm Trilogy*. That violence is unleashed in part through what might be described as the increase in the internal labour markets of crime: people renting out specific skills without any necessary connections to the overall purpose of a crime. What is important here is not that these marketable skills were suddenly introduced in the late twentieth century but that crime, as has been the case for other forms of paid labour, became increasingly specialist in its needs. Faced with what appears to be a contract killing, here is Wallender again:

> Wallender asked about the contract. As far as he was concerned, this was something new and frightening. Something that had only surfaced in the last few years, and then only in the three largest cities in the country. But before long it would be happening in his own back yard. Contracts were made between a customer and a professional killer, with the aim of murdering people. Pure and simple, a business deal: the ultimate proof that the brutalization of society had reached unfathomable depths.[28]

Those 'unfathomable depths' are the setting for the *Stockholm Trilogy*, a world in which the central characters pursue riches, largely through buying and selling drugs, with little or no thought not just for the human consequences but also for the moral boundaries that might need to be crossed. But this did not come without warning: as a policeman based in Stockholm says to Wallender:

> We're on the brink of losing control in Stockholm. I don't know how it is in a smaller district like Ystad but being a criminal in this city must be a pretty carefree existence, at least as far as the chances of getting caught are concerned.[29]

By the first decade of the twenty-first century what we are presented with in this detective fiction is a perception both an increase in the violence of crime but also the focus of that violence. In much of Mankell's fiction the adversaries are those of the police versus the criminal; the shift in Lapidus is to that of criminal versus criminal, with the police in some ways reduced to the status of onlooker at the wars between criminal rivals.

Kurt Wallender does not live to see the violence explicit in The *Stockholm Trilogy* emerging in his home town. That violence, in Sweden as in other context, did not emerge from nowhere and its origins take us back to that condition of anomie suggested as a condition of the modern and explored by various writers throughout the twentieth century. Being apart from a community, being alone is—as suggested above—both a feared and an admired quality of the twenty-first century. But how to belong, and to be a part of any group, remains as problematic as ever and is precisely the central personal issue confronted by the characters envisioned by Lapidus. What is crucially important here is that both these characters, in very different ways, are products of form of exclusion increasingly characteristic of the twenty-first century. Here is our introduction to Johan Westland:

> No one in the posh parts of Stockholm knew the following about Johan Westland, alias JW. He was an ordinary citizen, a loser, A tragic Sven. JW pretended to be an ultrabrat. Really, he was the world's biggest penny pinching pauper.[30]

What follows this is a description of the various ways in which JW saves money and does everything he possibly can do in order to pass as a member of the brat pack of rich young Swedish men.

This is not just another tale about a young man seduced by money; what JW wants is to buy the appearance of class; he could be read as yet another Jay Gatsby—Scott Fitzgerald's depiction of a penniless young man determined to buy his way into what he sees as 'high society'. The similarity between the fate of Gatsby and that of JW is that neither man manages to pass as a member of the exclusive world of 'old' money. Both discover that 'class' cannot be bought. But the difference between the two men is that of the lengths to which both will go to secure their ambitions, a different toleration of physical violence. Over the three volumes of the *Stockholm Trilogy*, JW's various fortunes include making and losing money, a spell in prison and various literally bruising encounters with parts of the global networks of the drugs trade. JW survives but here he is in the final volume of the trilogy, facing—and failing—a test of his class credentials:

> He fumbled for his knife and fork. Glances around the table to see which bread plate was his. Wiped his mouth too frequently with the

linen napkin… A truth was crystallising. No outsider could ever enter the world he was from… It was impossible. Entrance: barred. You would never become one of them for real. Because they were like a family. You wouldn't fool anyone with perfect table manners, the correct right-wing political sympathies or condescending comments about the plebs.[31]

What the *Stockholm Trilogy* tells us about is not just about the condition and the possibility of anomie. That, as suggested, is an inherent part of the modern world. But it does something more. It names the ways in which perceptions of isolation and exclusion are created and lived. The sources of JW's sense of exclusion are not, as is the case for the other central character Jorge Barrio, derived from realities of migration and legalities around citizenship but are about what appears to be the absolute impossibility of ever belonging to a world which is both materially and symbolically wealthy. The group to which JW aspires—the 'old' money of Swedish society—lives and dresses in ways which demand money. But as JW discovers to his cost, to be able to adopt the appearance of wealth is very far from being accepted. The monied class which JW wishes to belong to is eager to embrace JW's financial skills but what it is not willing to do is to recognise JW as 'one of them'.

JW, however, has gambled everything on belonging to the world of the rich. It is a world which is informed by fantasies about wealth and the goods that wealth can buy. It is not just a fantasy about getting rich, but also about being able to buy the 'signs' of success and taste. The *Stockholm Trilogy*, and the account of JW's ambitions, are littered with the names of expensive clothes and those objects and services which are heavily coded as exclusive. In all JW wants to acquire the symbolic sign of money quite as much as the money itself. In this he is a character as characteristic of consumer capitalism as the characters of Christie or Hammett were creatures of a capitalist world committed to accumulation. This, of course, poses new questions about the motives for crime in the twenty-first century, an emergent shift in moral values that Kurt Wallender had pondered over at the end of the twentieth century:

I live in a country where we've been taught to believe that all truths are simple, he thought. And also, that the truth is clear and unassailable. Our legal system is based on that principle. Now I'm starting to realise that the truth is complicated, multi- faceted, contradictory. That lies are both black and white. If one's view of humans, of human life, is disrespectful and contemptuous, then truth takes on another aspect than if life is regarded as inviolable.[32]

Later Wallender novels by Mankell continue this theme. But by the time that the first volume of the *Stockholm Trilogy* was published what had been firmly established about much of the west was first, continuing and increasing social inequality, second, the power of a culture of consumption and third a general access to global forms of communication. The mobile phone communications network which has made such inroads on forms of social communication began in Scandinavia and Wallander is of a generation which did not grow up with this form of technology. Like other colleagues, including Rebus, he continues to struggle with many of its aspects.[33]

But what Wallender—and many people of his age—had also grown up with, especially for the middle class, were worlds of secure employment and assured forms of state support. They had little or no experience of the way of life of a younger generation; Wallender himself often finds the life lived by his daughter Linda both incomprehensible and problematic. Although Wallender is eventually pleased that his daughter has followed him into the police force, and has at last settled into a permanent job, he cannot but help continuing to regard her attitudes and aspects of her way of life as at the best strange and at the worst unacceptable. An ancient problem of generations occurs: Wallender had problems with his father's values and behaviour. In his turn he and his daughter regard each other with continuing affection but across decades of difference.

Wallender lives in a world of various forms of separation between the generations. In this, it is notable that the murder with which *The White Lioness* begins is that of an entirely conventional woman, living an entirely conventional life. What is being murdered, we might conjecture, is not just this unfortunate person but the very manner of life which had been hers and yet can no longer be taken for granted. Industrial capitalism has always had to depend upon new products and new markets in order to survive. But what we see between *The White Lioness* and the *Stockholm Trilogy* is the appearance of a new commodity—that of various forms of recreational drugs—that is at odds with social norms and yet an integral part of the culture that provides constant vitality for consumption. As the young people who JW wishes to join make clear, the moral boundaries of consumption are now increasingly porous.

Yet those boundaries also include—as JW has found to his cost—rigid patterns of class inclusion and exclusion. These patterns are in many ways as rigorous and as well policed as any in the past. Most fundamentally, those boundaries exclude immigrants to Sweden—'Fortress Europe' keeps a tight watch on the movement of people. Jorge Barrio would, of course never be allowed into the same social spaces to which JW has a clearly conditional and fleeting access. JW is allowed into these groups if he can be useful, but otherwise he remains in exactly the same situation as the literal servants of a previous era: valued for their usefulness but otherwise apart. However, into these fiercely maintained boundaries in the real world has come a new development of the twenty-first century and one which Scandinavian detective fiction has been the first to explore fully: the internet and its policies. Stieg Larsson's *Millennium Trilogy* made it clear that the pathway to both knowledge about, and the control of, the world of the twenty-first century is competence at computing. JW, in common with Lisbeth Salander the heroine of the *Millennium Trilogy* is superbly competent in this dark art of the contemporary world. Even more competent in Larsson's fiction is the figure of Plague, the socially reclusive man who is even further ahead than Salander at the manipulation of the world from his keyboard. Under Plague's skilled fingers huge amounts of money appear and disappear, reputations are made and ruined and danger discovered and averted.

Plague has achieved something which has become, for many millions, an almost impossible goal: he can control aspects of the world. What he takes for granted is something which has increasingly attracted the attention of contemporary political scientists: what is described as the 'democratic deficit' of the twenty-first century. At first this judgment may seem rooted in historical ignorance, to suppose that the past in any European country was somehow a paradise of collective political engagement and agency. However, the named deficit is less about this fantasy than in the growing consensus that political decisions which affect millions of people are made less by the named institutions and practices of democracy (parliaments, voting, community associations) and more by unnamed and, crucially, unaccountable global corporations. The stranglehold of these institutions on the ordinary, everyday life of populations diminishes the sense that there are secure spaces, protected by the state and publicly visible individuals, which will afford protection and care. It is this apparently unknowable location of power that is the focus of the final novel to be discussed here, Ian Rankin's *Let it Bleed*. Rankin was, as he is the first to admit, hugely influenced by the three detective novels of William McIlvanney. The three detective novels which McIlvanney published between 1977 and 1991 (*Laidlaw*, *The Papers of Tony Veitch* and *Strange Loyalties*) have been hailed as the origin of 'tartan noir'.[34] The novels all feature a detective named Jack Laidlaw and the creation of the 'dark' side of Scotland, a side that Rankin is to extend to a wider culture and a wider range of institutions. Not least of the differences between the two authors is that Rankin writes of Edinburgh, the site of Scottish government and Anglicised convention. McIlvanney on the other hand sets his novels in Glasgow, a city long associated with a vibrant and often politically radical culture. The similarities between the work of the two authors are many but Rankin is, perhaps, the author who takes on both a wider definition of the 'political' and a greater scepticism about all forms of authority.

We see Inspector John Rebus in Rankin's *Let it Bleed* pitted against not just one wicked person but against an entire structure of power in Scotland. The novel was published at the point when the UK government of the time, with John Major as Prime Minister, was mired in accusations of corruption, deception and incompetence. The point that Rankin is making, and which is central to Chapter 2, is that no one individual is uniquely to blame; the problem is structural, the system is flawed. Towards the end of the novel Rebus has realised that he is unlikely to bring a powerful, and collectively guilty, group of men to anything approaching either condemnation or justice. Rankin writes of Rebus's views of the men he has been pursuing:

> They knew the way the world worked; they knew who - or rather what - was in charge. It wasn't the police or the politicians, it wasn't anyone stupid enough to place themselves in the front line. It was secret, quiet men who got on with their work the world over, bribing where necessary, breaking the rules, but quietly, in the name of 'progress', in the name of the 'system'.[35]

Such concerns are etched into the very DNA of the detective novel of the twenty-first century. From Wallender's growing disillusion with the procedures and the possibilities of policing to the much more radical rejection of forms of law and policing in Larsson and Lapidus we see the growing disquiet at the social project of maintaining boundaries between inside and outside the law. This scepticism, if not outright refusal, of the structural enforcement of justice is there in the desolate small towns of the novels by Karin Fossum, as much as in the sprawling and de-centred Glasgow of Malcolm Mackay, the housing estate of Tana French's *Broken Harbour* and the Belfast of Adrian McKinty: Most recently, a detective in Stav Sherez's *Eleven Days* remarks that: 'We have to face up to the fact people don't trust our laws any more....A disillusion with the prevailing structures of law government the likes of which we haven't seen before'.[36] This fiction, and much more by other authors, captures the effects on individuals and communities of living in the capitalism of the twenty-first century. Most strikingly those effects are of the desolation of shared, civic space and the relative proliferation of spaces, both physical and virtual, which are beyond control. The inefficiency, and the ineffectiveness of the state and its administrative agencies in protecting its citizens serves as an important backdrop to this. In sketching out this social world detective fiction poses the pressing question of what happens to individuals when there is no protection. In this world the resolution of a detective novel—as in the days of Christie—does not end with a happy marriage or a secure re-configuration of an imagined space but with only uncertainty and the lingering, but powerful, suspicion that other bad things will continue.

Notes

1. For a contemporary discussion of Lombroso's work, see Charles A. Ellwood, 'Lombroso's Theory of Crime', *Journal of Criminal Law and Criminology*, Vol. 2, Issue 5, 1912, pp. 716–23.
2. Lauren Berlant, *Cruel Optimism* (Durham, NC, Duke University Press, 2011) and Sara Ahmed, *The Cultural Politics of Emotion* (London, Routledge, 2013).
3. George Orwell, 'The Decline of the English Murder', *Tribune*, February 15, 1946.
4. Ian Watt set out the emergence of the major characteristics of the novel in *The Rise of the Novel* (London, Chatto and Windus, 1957).
5. The title of the 'first' European detective novel is contested. Edgar Allen Poe's *The Murder in the Rue Morgue* of 1841 is often cited, as is William Godwin's *Things as They Are or, The Adventures of Caleb Williams* (1794). Voltaire's *Zadig* (1748) is often named as an important influence on Poe. Outside Europe the story of 'The Three Apples' in the *Arabian Nights* is also often cited. The first English translation of this story appeared in 1845.
6. The Cathal Breen and Helen Tozer novels by William Shaw are *A Song from Dead Lips* (2013), *A House of Knives* (2014), *A Book of Scars* (2015) and *Sympathy for the Devil* (2017). All published by Quercus, London. *The Stockholm Trilogy* by Jens Lapidus consists of three volumes: *Easy Money* (2012), *Never Screw Up* (2013) and *Life Deluxe* (2014). All published by Macmillan, London.
7. Poirot first appeared in *The Mysterious Affair at Styles* by Agatha Christie, published in 1920.
8. Jane Martin, 'Beyond Suffrage: Feminism, Education and the Politics of Class in the Inter-War Years', *British Journal of the Sociology of Education*, Vol. 29, Issue 4, 2008, pp. 411–23.
9. Anna Maria Sigmund, *Women of the Third Reich* (Ontario, NDA Publishing, 2000).
10. Angus Calder, *The People's War* (London, Panther, 1971).
11. Penny Summerfield, *Women Workers in the Second World War* (London, Routledge, 2014) and Penny Summerfield and Corinna Peniston-Bird, *Contesting Home Defence: Men, Women and the Home Guard in the Second World War* (Manchester, Manchester University Press, 2007).

12. There are various accounts of the 1960s from various points on the political spectrum. See E.J. Hobsbawm, *Age of Extremes: A Short History of the Twentieth Century* (London, Michael Joseph, 1994), Chapters 10 and 11 and Avner Offer, *The Challenge of Affluence* (Oxford, Oxford University Press, 2006).

13. Selina Todd, *The People: The Rise and Fall of the Working Class* (London, John Murray, 2015), p. 8.

14. See Danny Dorling, *Inequality and the 1%* (London, Verso, 2014) and Tom Clark, with Anthony Heath, *Hard Times: Inequality, Recession, Aftermath* (London and New Haven, Yale University Press, 2014).

15. Luc Boltanski, *The New Spirit of Capitalism* (London, Verso, 2006).

16. John Bew, *Citizen Clem: A Biography of Attlee* (Oxford, Oxford University Press, 2017), p. xix.

17. Amongst novels which have included imprisonment one of the most vivid is Jussi Adler-Olsen, *Mercy* (London, Penguin, 2011).

18. The April/May revelations about the mis-use of personal data in both the UK Brexit vote and the 2016 USA Presidential Election were the most recent examples of this contemporary phenomenon. But the possibility had long been recognised. See (eds.) Wayne Le Cheminant and John M. Parnish, *Manipulating Democracy: Democratic Theory, Political Psychology and the Mass Media* (London and New York, 2011).

19. The BBC documentary was a three-part programme entitled *Three Girls*, directed by Phillipa Lowthorpe and shown over three weeks in May 2017.

20. Detective novels set in Iceland are particularly representative of narratives of 'uncovering'. See, for example, Arnaldur Indriðason, *Oblivion* (London, Vintage, 2014) and Yrsa Sigurðardóttir, *Ashes to Dust* (London, Hodder, 2012).

21. The ten volume Martin Beck series by Maj Sjöwall and Per Wahlöö was published between 1965 and 1975. For a review essay on their work and details of secondary literature see Katarina Gregersdotter in (ed.) Barry Forshaw, *Detective* (Bristol and Chicago, Intellect Books, 2016), pp. 44–55.

22. One of the most famous, and the most committed to both detective novels and Christianity, was T.S. Eliot. See the essay by Paul Grimstad, 'What Makes Great Detective Fiction: According to T.S. Eliot' in the *New Yorker*, February 2, 2016.

23. Keith Thomas, *Religion and the Decline of Magic* (Harmondsworth, Penguin, 1971).

24. The first most important statement of scepticism about the European Enlightenment was *Dialectic of Enlightenment*, by Theodor Adorno and Max Horkheimer, first published in German in 1944. For an English translation see the 1997 edition published by Verso, London.

25. Ed McBain wrote a total of 83 novels in the 87th Precinct series, all of them demonstrating the worth and the integrity of the New York Police Department.

26. Selina Todd, p. 68.

27. Henning Mankell, *The White Lioness* (London, Vintage, 2012), p. 23.

28. *The White Lioness*, p. 185.

29. *The White Lioness*, p. 202.

30. Jens Lapidus, *Easy Money* (London, Pan, 2014), p. 46.

31. Jens Lapidus, *Life Deluxe* (London, Pan, 2014), p. 466.

32. *The White Lioness*, p. 247.

33. Ian Rankin, *Let it Bleed* (London, Orion, 1996), p. 327.

34. W. McIlvanney, *Laidlaw* (London, Hodder and Stoughton, 1977); *The Papers of Tony Veitch* (London, Hodder and Stoughton, 1983); and *Strange Loyalties* (London, Hodder and Stoughton, 1991).

35. Ian Rankin, Let it Bleed (London, Orion, 1995), p. 357.

36. Stav Sherez, *Eleven Days* (London, Faber and Faber, 2013).

3

Who's to Blame?

Who's to Blame?

Blame is a pressing concern for all societies. Or, more specifically, the question of how to allocate blame, how to contain and direct it, is an enduring concern. The earliest records of human history suggest as much. Take, for example, the ancient code of Hammurabi and the Icelandic sagas, each of them offering a fascinating insight into early social mechanisms for accusing, adjudicating, and punishing wrong-doers.[1] How a society decides these matters tells us much about how it operates, not least of all how power is instituted and legitimated.

Today, in late modern societies, blame is a source of radical contestation and deep discontent. 'Whodunnit?' has become the refrain for our age, just as—perhaps it should be 'because'—the bases for determining who did what, to whom have come to seem increasingly unreliable. This chapter explores these ideas, and in doing so extends the work of Chapter 1 in establishing the 'scene of the crime', that is, the broad social, political, and economic context of the post-1970s period that we believe is so vividly brought to life in detective fiction. Here, our concern is with the post-1970s epistemological shift in how we have come

© The Author(s) 2019
M. Evans et al., *Detecting the Social*, https://doi.org/10.1007/978-3-319-94520-0_3

to view truth, knowledge, and authority—what is often referred to as the postmodern turn.[2] Sociologists tend to agree that the result of this cultural transformation is greater uncertainty about events and people, who we can rely on for the 'truth', and the bases for claims about 'reality'. In the world of the post-1970s detective novel, these philosophical matters are also deeply social: we are consistently shown that the frustration of not knowing for sure is linked to the problem of corruption, broadly conceived. There is always, in this fiction, a 'bigger picture' that is in turns obscured and revealed. What works to conceal this set of deeper truths is an often-elaborate act of misdirection on the part of those with power, so that blame is cast on those who can be easily construed as dangerous. The standard victims in post-1970s detective fiction are left, then, with a particular kind of uncertainty about the truth, one that is the basis for an acute sense of loss and anger. They serve to remind us of what's at stake in deducing what went wrong, who did it, and why.

Take, by way of example, *Calling Out for You*, a 2006 novel by the Norwegian writer Karin Fossum. Here, we are asked to think about the space we make in our lives for other people, and the gaping holes that are left when they depart. We start the novel by following Gunder Jomann as he prepares for the arrival of Poona, his new bride, due to arrive soon from India. Gunder, we learn, is middle-aged, gentle, and a man of habit. His neighbours and friends were surprised by his decision to go travelling in India. The fact that he returned a married man is big news indeed in this remote Norwegian town. We find out about all this later: what we start with is Gunder carefully and quietly cleaning, stocking up, refurnishing, and adjusting his living arrangements in anticipation of Poona's arrival, and thinking about what he's clearing the way for: the colour and energy of his new wife, and a fuller life.

But Poona never arrives. Her body is found, days past her arrival date, unceremoniously dumped in a nearby field. The community is horrified, but tight-lipped about the event. Almost everyone would rather the whole thing was forgotten about. There wasn't really room for Poona in this close-knit Norwegian community anyway. The out-of-town detectives interview everyone—it's a small place—and *no one saw anything*. But, of course, they did. They noticed the telling details that life-long members of small communities are apt to see: a car driving a little bit faster than usual, someone trying to conceal an injured arm, and a slight frostiness between two people who usually get along. The investigators perceive these to be clues, but their deeper meaning—and thus what they evidence—remains unavailable to them. So, although someone is eventually charged with Poona's murder, the version of events we're offered to explain what happened doesn't really hold water. The detectives aren't really sure they got their man, either.

In so many ways, *Calling Out for You* distils the concerns of post-1970s detective fiction. For one thing, it's interested in how local communities are disrupted by and respond to global forces—here, and elsewhere, migration from the global South to the global North. Chapter 1 was partly concerned with establishing such concerns as a distinguishing feature of the genre, post-1970s. The novel also shares with recent detective fiction an important structural feature: a lack of resolution. Fossum vividly captures someone clearing-out his life in readiness for it to become complete, denies the realisation of this, and then refuses to offer a satisfying compensation for that loss. It's a story arc that is familiar to any avid reader of contemporary detective fiction. A notable amount of post-1970s detective novels end without a culprit being discovered or with the guilty party going free. Yet more end with a deep sense that those really responsible have somehow escaped justice. The serialised format of most detective fiction is key to this effect. Serialisation has always been a feature of the genre,[3] and with this comes the possibility for story-lines spanning across books or television series, and for character or action to be developed across discrete episodes. We tend to start each Agatha Christie novel, for example, with the same central characters, applying their skills of detection to a fresh case and a new ensemble cast of suspects. Serialisation here works to confirm Poirot or Miss Marple's intellectual agility and flexibility. By contrast, much of today's detective fiction starts with an ostensibly fresh case that then leads us back to the same old set of elusive suspects or criminal organisations that escaped capture last time round. Take Jo Nesbø's *The Redbreast* (2000), *Nemesis* (2002), and *The Devil's Star* (2003)—often seen as a trilogy within his longer Harry Hole series— where the search for a corrupt police officer-come-criminal underworld boss serves as a central thread running across the novels. Serialisation, here, works to confirm that locating and rooting-out wrong-doers is a problem of epic (rather than episodic) proportions.

The frustration of unclear or delayed endings reflects a more general problem posed in post-1970s detective fiction, and that is the sheer difficulty in definitively working out 'who did this bad thing'. In the world of the contemporary detective novel, these frustrations are intimately bound up with the operation of power. We soon learn that some have the ability to control, directly and indirectly, the official narrative around 'what happened' and who should take the blame. Crucially, contemporary detective fiction points out that the mis-allocation of blame is socially-patterned, rather than random. If the fall-guy, the scapegoat, and the stitch-up are recurrent features of these stories, they also, almost inevitably, tell us something about the inexorable flow of blame, from those who are powerful enough to direct an accusation, towards individuals who are so powerless as to be easily made into a patsy. Think, for one moment, about the typical victims of wrongful accusations in post-1970s detective fiction: they include people who are homeless, those with a history of institutionalisation, petty thieves, people with a mental disability, the young, and the disaffected.

We come back to this point in due course. For now, we want to point out that the problem of unclear endings in post-1970s detective fiction reflects—and tells us much about—a cultural shift in the relationship between blame and responsibility. We might frequently lump these two terms together, and for good reason, as we come to below, but their meaning is quite distinct. Blame is the older term, originating in the twelfth century, and comes from the French verb *blamer* (to rebuke, criticise, condemn). Blame is something that a person or group allocates to another, and it makes an explicit call for external, collective agreement. Responsibility is the newer word: it originates at the turn of the sixteenth century, comes again from the French, and refers to someone being answerable for a deed.[4] It's an idea that more obviously belongs to the modern social world, where people come to be seen as intentional actors, the originators of ideas and beliefs, rather than the conveyors of God's will or subject to supernatural forces. Responsibility is something that is allocated on the basis of a forensic examination of someone's role in an event or act, and that's because it infers causation. To accept responsibility means acknowledging that something you did caused something to happen (or, that something you *didn't* do was instrumental in an event—but more on that towards the end of the chapter).

For the greater part of human history, and prior to modernity, declarations of blame did not require the allocation of responsibility, as we understand it today. The law, for example, offered greater protection from blame to free men, and particularly those of the upper social classes, and this was irrespective of their responsibility for an event.[5] And those deemed inherently dangerous—nonconforming women and itinerants, amongst others—were frequently blamed for events that were then mysterious in their causes, such as droughts and lethal storms.

This makes it all the more notable that in detective fiction right up until the last quarter of the twentieth century, blame and responsibility tend to coincide. In fact, this relationship is absolutely crucial to much early and Golden Age detective fiction. Think, for one moment, about the standard device in these novels of finishing with the detective calling in the group of suspects to offer up a detailed explanation of what happened. This narrative structure, so familiar to fans of Christie, Sayers, or Chesterton, serves both as a means of locating responsibility and allocating blame. And if this device puts us in mind of the modern courtroom—the assembled characters serving as a makeshift jury, the detective reconstructing what happened, the culprit ceremoniously dispatched into police custody—that's because here, too, responsibility and blame are firmly knitted together. More on that below. For now, we want to point out that a notable feature of post-1970s detective fiction is the pulling apart of blame and responsibility, as well as a radical contestation of the relevance of each of these ideas to contemporary problems of crime and justice. This is by no means a novel feature of contemporary detective fiction; Carlo Emilio Gadda's (1957) novel *That Awful Mess on the* Via *Merulana* was an important precursor to today's stories of complicated, unclear lines of responsibility. It's reasonable to suggest, though, that post-1970s detective fiction has engaged in an especially thoroughgoing consideration of the nature of and relationship between responsibility and blame.

Take, again, Fossum's *Calling out to You*: here someone is blamed, but there is substantial doubt about whether this is the person who is really responsible for the act. To boot, we're asked to consider the distinct possibility that the person charged with the crime is merely a victim of pernicious ideas about loners. At the same time—and this is one of the achievements of Fossum's novel—it's clear that blame remains an important institutional outcome. Settling the question of 'whodunnit?' matters greatly to individuals and a community. We're asked to weigh this against the risk of allocating blame too quickly, too conveniently.

In other post-1970s detective novels, we're asked to consider the possibility that the person who is responsible for an act isn't to blame. Lisbeth Salander, Stieg Larsson's protagonist in his *Millennium Trilogy*, is certainly responsible for assaulting her legal guardian Nils Bjurman, but we can hardly *blame* her for seeking revenge on a man who has raped her, especially since the social agencies responsible for protecting her have failed so spectacularly. A striking number of Henning Mankell's novels in his Kurt Wallander series focus too on crimes perpetrated by those who have suffered a terrible injustice (whether that's an enraged daughter seeking revenge for her mother's unpunished murder in *The Fifth Woman*, or the young man hunting down those involved in a human trafficking ring in *Side-tracked*). Here, and elsewhere, post-1970s detective fiction suggests that the official allocation of blame is just one permutation—and, with striking regularity, only those who are ready to accept this can get anywhere near the truth of the situation. In this way, this body of fiction proposes a new way of thinking about blame, where a range of actors are indirectly responsible for (and therefore implicated in) a bad thing happening, and where those most at fault find ways to foist responsibility onto others. If postmodern skepticism about ultimate causes allows us to entertain the former idea, it's distrust of authority and power that provides the basis for the latter.

This chapter sets out to unpack these features of post-1970s detective fiction and consider what this tells us about popular conceptions of crime and justice. Before that, though, we want to acknowledge the fact that there are a large number of contemporary detective novels where allocating blame and responsibility is rather more clear-cut. Extraordinarily so, in fact. We're thinking here about forensic police procedural fiction, such as Patricia Cornwell's novels featuring Kay Scarpetta, Kathy Reichs' Tempe Brennan series, and Tess Gerritsen's Rizzoli & Isles series. This brand of fiction has become particularly popular since 1990, buoyed, no doubt, by the incredible global success of the *CSI: Crime Scene Investigation* television franchise. Here, there is comfort to be found in the fact that scientific techniques of criminal profiling, analysis of human traces (notably, DNA-testing), as well as computer-assisted technology in searching huge databases, can uncover the absolute truth of the situation. There are no questions about the epistemological, empirical, or moral bases for blame and responsibility here. The favouring of clear, tidy endings in this sub-genre is helped by the tendency for perpetrators to be psychopathic, or otherwise suffering from a severe mental disturbance. In these cases, actions have no deeper meaning, and we're rarely made aware of any prior, pre-disposing experiences or events that might muddy the water when it comes to allocating responsibility and blame.

Still, when we think more carefully about forensic police procedural fiction, we might notice that what at first glance looks like limitless faith in techniques of contemporary detection to determine responsibility is rather more complicated. We're reminded here of Deleuze's (2004, originally 1966) argument about the French crime novel series, *La Série Noire*. Deleuze points out that literary detectives in this set of novels depend, to an alarming degree, on accidental discoveries and slip-ups. By way of comparison, he points out that early twentieth century detective novels, in both the British and French tradition, depend upon the balletic intellectual leaps of the detective-protagonist. For Deleuze, the newer brand of detective fiction reflects a fundamental cultural misgiving about human powers of deduction and induction.

A similar point can be made about more recent police procedurals that fasten upon the forensic techniques of detection. After all, detectives in these stories don't solve a case using their critical faculties of human judgement: technology and science does that work instead. In fact, forensic tools appear better equipped than humans to do the work of detection: they 'see' more clearly than humans (both in a physical sense, and by virtue of seeming to lack bias), and can process swathes of data with greater speed and accuracy. So, like the post-1970s detective novels that form the focal point of this book, forensic police procedurals suggest that there are fundamental insufficiencies with human forms of investigation and judgement.

Or, more specifically, the implication in both forms of detective fiction, is that *police*-led investigation and judgement is a problem. Here it's worth pausing to note a key shift in detective novels of the last century away from a focus on the work of privately hired detectives, and towards police work. For the critical German social theorists of the early-mid twentieth century, the value of the detective novel came from its crystallisation of a specific form of rationality. So, Bloch, Brecht, Benjamin and Kracauer all immediately reach for the metaphor of the puzzle to describe the structure and appeal of the early detective novel, and that's because these novels are fundamentally about an *individual* mode of thinking.[6] In contrast, police procedural fiction is sociologically fascinating for its rendering of a certain type of *institutional* thinking.

This form of institutional thinking has its roots in the early to mid-nineteenth century, and it's worth devoting some space here to considering its bases and key features. Certain parts of this argument are well-rehearsed, not least of all by Foucault (1991). Modernity gave rise to a certain conception and discourse of crime and criminal justice—to the idea of punishment as a social corrective and criminal detection as a specific job, involving disinterested examination of the facts. Lacey (2012) points out that, criminal intention increasingly came to be seen in terms of a discrete course of action, separable (formally, at least) from being a troublemaker, scoundrel, or *wrong 'un*. Thus, as Lacey (2012) observes, the new evidentiary trial of the nineteenth century came to focus, ostensibly, at least, on conduct as a means of deciding someone's character, rather than the other way round—and, we might add, it was (and remains) decisive, intentional conduct that mattered. This meant, amongst other things, that the criminal trial became more lawyer-led, and the messy, emotional testimony of witnesses became increasingly marginal to court proceedings (Rabin 2004).[7] Around these concrete shifts in practice we can observe a broader, more gradual and socially entrenched shift in the meaning of justice, deviance, and social order. That is, steadily, the institution of criminal justice—'the law', we might colloquially say, but we mean so much more than that—became the main frame of reference for discussions about morality, blame, and restitution. And it's worth noting here that, despite regional and national variation, we can think of this as a pan-European shift. Lenman and Parker's (1980) ambitious work of criminal justice history points to the slow dissolution of loose community legal structures across the European continent during the early modern period, and their eventual replacement with state-wide legal apparatus, and modern, bureaucratic criminal justice systems.

This is a view of the emergence of modern criminal justice that obscures back-steps and contradictions, uneasy alliances and fierce battles over meaning. What this broad view of criminal justice provides, though, is a sense of wholesale institutional change, at the heart of which was the idea that the criminal act and intention (schematically conceived) are the proper foci for official investigation. How are we to understand the emergence of this institutional thinking? For one thing, as Lacey (2012) indicates modern criminal justice answered to the problems of traceability, knowability, and belonging that were intrinsic to modern society. The turn towards a more forensic treatment of the criminal and his conduct—and, importantly, conduct ahead of character—reflected the needs of a more mobile, urban population. Urban sociologists often point out that one of the effects of mass urbanisation on everyday life was that it made people harder to 'read' and place, partly because so much of the social interaction within a city is fleeting and anonymous, and partly because of increased social and cultural differentiation (Lofland 1973; Sennett 1993).

That modern criminal justice sought to approach each defendant as an unknown—and as knowable through deed alone—reflected not just a desire to attend to matters of truth with scientific objectivity, but also the declining importance of durable social relations and character as social resources (Lacey 2012). To put it differently, in the village community the question of 'Who did this bad thing?' is efficiently answered by recourse to a shared understanding of people's characters; in the city, there is no such shared community knowledge to draw upon, and so the question can only be answered by focussing on the act of wrongdoing, tracing suspects' movement, and ascertaining the effects of individuals' actions. As Lacey (2012) argues this is a world where the logic of responsibility reigns.

It is also a world where crime comes to be seen as a discrete social problem requiring formal intervention. Much has been written about this in a UK context, where the early onset of industrialisation and mass urbanisation gave particular urgency to the idea of a distinct 'criminal' or 'dangerous' class (Emsley 2005: 68). Technical expertise was a key feature of this supposed new class, and Churchill (2016) points to the role of nineteenth century UK security firms in conjuring up the problem of the skilled, tech-savvy criminal—a forerunner, we might reasonably suggest, to today's hackers and phishers, as they are popularly-conceived. These ideas about the problem of criminality will be familiar to anyone who's read a Charles Dickens' novel. That Dickens saw his fiction as a platform for promoting social reform is well known, and one of the problems he takes aim at is crime as an effect of urban, working class degradation. Others are capable of crime in Dickens' novels, but their involvement is more likely to be framed in terms of an out of character error of judgement than a predilection for crime. Dickens' protagonists tend to err, but they are not meant for a life of crime: they learn, they move on, they make amends. What tends to make the difference between these redeemable individuals and the darkly-criminal gangs of London—*Oliver Twist* brings the latter to life especially well—is education, and, with it, that most vague of attributes: a good character.

Dickens doesn't quite give into the idea that certain people are born to be bad, but there is nonetheless a persistent suggestion in his novels that social class background serves as a type of predestination.[8] For some, this was a persuasive idea. It was precisely this assumption that informed the new positivist criminology that emerged in Italy during the early nineteenth century and was then taken up elsewhere in Europe. Cesare Lombroso, often seen as the originator of this school of thought, collected masses of biological data on convicted criminals, with a view to arriving at a profile of the criminal as a physical type. It's a project that is now widely derided, not least of all because, as most contemporary criminologists point out, individuals belonging to certain social groups are disproportionately stopped, pursued, arrested, and convicted of criminal offences. Lombroso, in other words, was only studying those who the law, police, and courts deemed criminal, and that's ignoring the fact that his work of measuring and recording failed to reveal any reliable patterns.

It's tempting to see positivist criminology as harkening back to ancient ideas about dangerous individuals, but this misses what's distinctively modern about the perspective. Lombroso's project was self-consciously scientific, his aim to study, rationally and methodically, the problem of criminality. In this sense, he seemed to offer a powerful confirmation that those belonging to the urban working class were 'born' criminal. In doing so, he answered to the same fears concerning city-life and others' unknowability as the modern criminal justice system, in its emphasis on criminal intention and action. After all, Lombroso's project also aimed to locate the problem of crime.

These ideas about human nature and criminality were by no means restricted to the realm of fantasy, nor to the nineteenth century. In the 1920s, a set of libel cases involving Edith Swan and Rose Gooding reveals that the deep connection between social class, morality, and perceived criminality lasted into the first half of the twentieth century. The case, and the interpretation offered here, is detailed by Hilliard (2017). Swan and Gooding were neighbours in an English seaside town of Littlehampton, and each in turn was accused of sending poison pen letters—sweary, obscene, and anonymous—to members of the local community. Gooding, a working-class woman from a family renowned locally for causing trouble, spent two stretches of time in prison for the offence. Swan, a lower middle-class woman, religious, and of some education, was exonerated by the judge, despite the overwhelming evidence of her guilt, on the basis that a woman of her background was incapable of such a crime. Hilliard (2017) leaves us in no doubt that she was the culprit. And he also leaves us in no doubt of the role of social class in this case.

All of this is to point out that whilst we can determine some very important features of how the modern institution of criminal justice 'thinks', how it *acts* is often another matter. For at the very same time that the criminal justice system in the UK, and elsewhere, was developing to become more interested in conduct, rather than character, in practice, ideas about social class (and, we could add, gender and ethnicity) very much influenced how people were treated within that system.

This is a disjuncture that post-1970s detective fiction has, in various ways, sought to reveal and critique. In doing so, this body of literature indicates the declining purchase of criminal justice as a formal set of mechanisms for allocating responsibility and blame. Before thinking more deeply about all of this, let's start with what came before the fall—more particularly, the mid-twentieth century, a period when public trust in criminal justice, and the work of the state more generally, was significantly stronger than today.[9]

Nothing quite captures the distinctive purchase of criminal justice during the mid-twentieth century as Josephine Tey's (1951) novel, *The Daughter of Time*. Less widely known than her fellow British crime writers of the mid-twentieth century, Tey is nonetheless held in high esteem by many crime fiction enthusiasts, and her late novel *The Daughter of Time* is regularly seen as an important contribution to the genre. The novel's detective-protagonist is Detective Inspector Alan Grant. Here he is convalescing, staring listlessly at a hospital ceiling and desperately missing Scotland Yard. A friend brings him pictures of infamous historical villains and victims to scrutinise: she knows they'll be of interest to Grant because of the detective's long-standing faith in the idea that a man of judgement can immediately discern, just from looking, whether someone's a respectable character or a ne'er do well. It's in this batch of pictures that Grant finds his muse: Richard III—Holbein's portrait of him, at least.

Grant looks and looks; he can only see vulnerability in the portrait. This, he declares, is not the face of a man who murdered his two nephews to protect his claim to the crown (and we may well be reminded of another well-known painting here: Millais' *Princes in the Tower*, of the two young boys clothed in black and nervously clinging to one another). Proceeding from his hunch—very much a police detective's hunch about the face of evil—Grant turns to history books to assess the evidence for the king's misdemeanour and finds it to be frustratingly thin. The case against Richard is mired by hearsay, bias, and lazy presupposition. The account generally taken to be definitive, Grant finds, was written several decades after the event by a court historian with a vested interest in denouncing Richard as the murderer and reinforcing the rightfulness of Tudor ascension. History is found wanting here—at least, that is, by modern standards of proof, where blame has to follow not from the exigencies of political convenience, but from a cool-headed analysis of the facts.

Where History fails, criminal detection succeeds: that is very much the lesson of *The Daughter of Time*. Aided by a volunteer researcher—a young American carrying out research in the British Museum, whose nationality makes him immune to the convenient lies of British History—Grant reopens the case against Richard from his hospital bed. His focus is on the simple material facts of the event. He pieces together evidence from official records that indicate who was where, when. Proceeding in this manner, the case against Richard crumbles: there was nothing to suggest he knew the Princes were in the tower, nothing to link him to their death, and, anyway, he had no reason to kill the boys.

These are familiar to us, of course, as the regular foci for evidence in the detective story, and, indeed, modern criminal law: they concern the matters of prior knowledge, known movements and alibis, and motive, all of them empirically verifiable through material traces, impersonal bureaucratic records, and eyewitness testimony. These, the novel suggests, are the proper methods for detection and the proper bases for adjudication. One thing that's striking is how absolutely natural this approach is made to seem. 'Truth', the famous Francis Bacon maxim has it, is the 'daughter of time'; we're asked to see modern methods of criminal detection as simply (that is, neutrally, naturally, easily) facilitating an inevitable uncovering of the truth.

Criminal detection, in this book, not only triumphs in the narrow sense of substantiating an absence of guilt. By urging us to refashion our ideas about History's claim to truth and offering up a new version of our shared past, criminal detection is depicted here as peculiarly well-suited to deciding matters of truth and virtue in the real world. Detection saves the day in *The Daughter of Time*—that, of course, in line with what we expect of the detective novel. That it also urges us to reformulate our understanding of real-life events, British history, and our basis for understanding both is deeply suggestive of its cultural salience during the mid-twentieth century.

If Tey's novel stands as testament to post-war faith in official routes to justice, Stieg Larsson's *The Girl Who Kicked the Hornets' Nest* (2009) might be seen as a distillation of early twenty-first century anxiety about these precise same methods for establishing responsibility.[10] In *The Daughter of Time* police detection is strikingly efficient at getting at the truth; in *The Girl Who Kicked the Hornets' Nest* it is utterly inadequate in identifying the guilty party. The third in Larsson's *Millennium Trilogy*, the novel focuses on the murder trial of Lisbeth Salander. A ward of the state, Salander stands accused of murdering her guardian Nils Bjurman, as well as a rookie journalist and his girlfriend. She claims to know nothing about the latter two murders, but the material facts of the case are undeniable: Salander's fingerprints are all over the murder weapon, official police reports and psychiatric records demonstrate her propensity for violence, and eyewitness testimony places her at the scene of the crime. This is the basis for the prosecuting police's case against her. By means of defence, Salander produces a lengthy autobiography in which she alleges that she's the victim of a state-led cover up. The prosecuting police officers think she's utterly mad; the reader knows she's telling the truth. Salander's autobiography is meant as a provocation to her prosecutors: if you're looking for crime, you're looking at the wrong person and—more importantly—in the wrong place.

Comparing *The Daughter of Time* and *The Girl who Kicked the Hornets' Nest* illuminates a radical shift in the popular conception of detection, its method and principles, and in turn points to the changing relationship between responsibility and blame. Let's start with differences in method. The job of the police detective, Grant asserts throughout *The Daughter of Time*, is to register and then suppress their gut instincts about guilt, postpone judgement and embark upon a dispassionate assessment of the material evidence. Two things are of particular importance to this method of detection and central to the detective novel formula right up until the last quarter of the twentieth century: the idea that people's movements are traceable and that the detective is an unprejudiced investigator. The underlying presumption is that judgements about character can and should be postponed until someone's actions have been traced and verified. This ability to examine conduct ahead of deciding character is precisely what distinguishes Inspector Grant's re-investigation of Richard III, and other examples of effective detection in the genre. As Brecht observed, 'what is crucial' about the detective novel—in the mid-twentieth century, it bears reiterating—'is that the action is not developed from the characters, but the characters from the action'. This, then, is what distinguishes the early literary detective's gaze: by an effort of rationality he can push aside a visceral sense of moral indignation and postpone appraisals of character to examine the 'bare facts'. This, it might be added, is also a cherished principle of modern criminal law and was fundamental to the rationalisation of the legal system in England and Wales in the early-mid nineteenth century—it is, to go back to the discussion above, central to how criminal justice as a modern institution 'thinks'.

The police detectives of Larsson's *The Girl who Kicked the Hornets' Nest* ostensibly follow the same method of detection as Tey's Inspector Grant, in the sense that they undertake work in a routine and seemingly dispassionate fashion to ascertain the co-ordinates of time and space for the crime and chief suspect. Here, though, this approach is deeply dubious as a means of establishing the truth. First, we're urged to recognise that in working to prove a hypothesis—that Salander is the guilty party—the police investigators take too narrow a focus in terms of both the crime committed and the possibilities for blame. Whilst they work systematically and tirelessly to substantiate a particular version of a particular event, the real explanation for how these bad things came to happen becomes available to those ready to accept a messier, more open-ended story of collective blame.

Avid readers of detective novels may well feel compelled to point out here that Larsson's book is in keeping with the standard and long-standing depiction of police officers as bumbling idiots who, to put it bluntly, can't see for looking.[11] Certainly, nineteenth and early twentieth century literary detectives, amongst them Sherlock Holmes, C. Auguste Dupin, and Hercule Poirot, are often at pains to point out work-a-day police officers' lack of imagination in looking at a crime scene. The mistakes made by police officers in early detective fiction are, though, errors in looking-as-thinking, particularly in not seeing how a departure from everyday conduct and appearance—a non-barking dog, a clumsy word, a fussy hairdo—relates to a crime. In contrast, in much twenty-first century detective fiction, police officers' errors lie in problem-conception; in fastening, that is, on a particular act and suspect, and erroneously spinning evidence around them to elaborate a discrete chain of events. Here *the very idea of a crime scene*—that most important and primary unit of analysis in earlier detective novels—is contested, because to focus on working out what happened *here and only here* is to ignore the broader story for which this place may be just one setting. Put differently, in contemporary detective fiction we're often urged to think about the presumptions that precede and shape the process of looking-as-thinking. The critical question made of police detection is not, as is the case in earlier fiction, 'what have the cops failed to see here?' but rather 'why did they look here, and only here?' The distinction is crucial: the former question implies a deficiency of perception and logic, the latter a much more intractable problem of incorrect first principles in criminal detection. In Stieg Larsson's *The Girl Who Kicked the Hornets' Nest* what the police detectives principally miss is the bigger picture, rather than the telling details. It's worth emphasising here that this is by no means an abstract problem in Larsson's novel. The 'bigger picture' is vividly-sketched: it means, in this instance, the neglect of social services, medical malpractice, state corruption, an abusive father, and the possibility for a complicated collusion to misdirect blame.

The Girl Who Kicked the Hornets' Nest chimes with contemporary concerns. For one thing, it reflects a decline in public trust in social authorities across liberal democracies, partly a consequence of the new mood of scepticism about traditional sources of authority that emerged with the 1960s counter-culture.[12] And, crucially, this sense of distrust and disquiet was directed towards institutional arrangements. It was not merely, in other words, that the professionals entrusted with our care—doctors, social workers, police officers, amongst others—came to be seen as potentially untrustworthy, but that the processes and practices of medicine, social work, and criminal justice came to be seen as hopelessly flawed. In the world of the post-1970s detective novel, this scepticism has especially solid grounds. Here, social institutions are frequently found to be corrupt and, just as importantly, *unconsciously* sustain lies and repress the truth through a mixture of closed-mindedness, the privileging of certain views, and the silencing of others. This body of literature forces us to reflect upon the fact that only those with power can allocate blame, and formal assertions of blame tend to reinforce that power.

If post-1970s detective fiction asks us to be deeply suspicious of formal assertions of blame, it also urges us to think critically about claims surrounding responsibility. It does so by asking us to engage with a set of epistemological problems concerning the basis for truth-claims and the nature of evidence. In *The Girl Who Kicked the Hornets' Nest*, this constitutes another problem of method: the police detectives are hampered by an uncritical view of evidence that sees it as a straightforward re-telling of what happened. More broadly, post-1970s detective fiction asks us to think about the relationship between truth and knowledge, and in doing so raises crucial questions about the epistemological bases for assertions of responsibility. There's lots to say here. Let's start by observing that, in the world of much post-1970s detective fiction, material evidence is frequently concocted by those in power, and therefore deeply untrustworthy and liable to perpetuate problems of violence and corruption. As a result, it frequently seems as though the only really effective police work is done by those detectives who have been cast aside by regular police forces and operate as rogue agents. Jo Nesbø's Harry Hole is a case in point here, as are the outcast officers of Mick Herron's *Slow Horses* series. Herron does an especially effective job of sketching out a world where the failure of the police is not just a simple matter of corruption or ineptitude on the part of individuals but is instead systemic. In Herron's novels—set in twenty-first century London—the higher-ups of the Intelligence Service have a vested interest in maintaining, and at times aiding, serious and organised crime. Problems of law and order legitimise the existence of the police and secret services, and in a social world dominated by political spin and media hype, orchestrating situations that cast these social authorities in a positive light seems very appealing indeed. This is a social context where police work is driven by public relations—to perverse, farcical effect—and the real keepers of the peace are those police officers who operate at the margins, outside of the system.

In this context, it's interesting to note a trend for post-1970s detective fiction to be set during periods of significant social unrest and political turmoil. This allows for especially vivid depictions of criminal justice systems that are strained and unfit for purpose. Take, by way of example, Allan Massie's *Death in Bordeaux* series (set in Vichy Paris), Adrian McKinty's Sean Duffy series (set during the height of the Northern Irish 'Troubles'), and Michael Dibdin's Aurelio Zen series (set during a tumultuous period of Italian Mafia violence). Police corruption is a central theme here, as is—perhaps more interestingly—the consequences of institutional malaise, indifference, and inaction. The lesson of much of this literature is that the police don't attend to all crimes equally, and that in following orders to direct their skills of detection one way (and not in others), they are sustaining the social order, injustices and all. Nowhere is this clearer than in the recurring motif of the missing, redacted, empty, or prematurely closed case file. It's a vivid reminder that neglecting a case is itself a form of fabrication concerning what sorts of crime are officially allowed to exist and which sorts of people are permitted help.

There are other ways in which post-1970s detective fiction urges us to adopt a position of radical scepticism towards evidence, knowledge, and detection. Take, for example, the tendency—particularly since the turn of the twenty-first century—for central characters in these novels to have multiple personality disorders that render them deeply unreliable narrators or witnesses. Erik Axl Sund's *The Crow Girl* (2016) is a particularly interesting example of this, but we find the same device used in Nesbø's *The Redbreast* (2000), amongst others. The effect is to suggest that even interior monologues (that traditional source of 'real' knowledge in the novel) is something that the reader can't rely upon to reveal the reality of a situation.

None of this is to suggest that there is no way of knowing what happened in post-1970s detective fiction. It's just that the basis for 'real' knowledge is relatively restricted and open to contestation. The existence of multiple and contradictory 'voices' in a narration isn't necessarily a problem overall: in *The Crow Girl*, for example, it is the central character's disentangling of her various personae that leads to her working out what happened. Hearing *all* voices is one way of letting the truth come out.[13] In other instances, direct access to the guilty act is the central criterion for truth-claims. In a social world where traces of a guilty act are difficult to come by and official records are to be treated with cynicism, the only way you can know for sure is by seeking out a direct expression of guilt. Wrong-doers don't give themselves away in Stieg Larsson's novels, their acts aren't deduced and renounced, in the fashion of an Agatha Christie novel; we know of their guilt because we are made a witness to their bad deeds. Thus, the climax of Larsson's first novel is not the detective's reconstruction of events and denunciation, but the murderer's confession, made to the novel's detective-protagonist whilst he is tied-up and awaiting mutilation in the killer's torture chamber. In the final novel of the *Millennium Trilogy* Salander is found 'not guilty' largely on the basis of a film she surreptitiously made of her guardian raping her; and, it's worth noting that the reader has already witnessed this crime as it happened. The sub-plots of both the first and third novels—concerning, respectively, financial misdealing and anonymous threats made by email—reach their conclusion with Salander hacking a computer and finding the original material.

The implication throughout the trilogy is that evidence is to be mistrusted unless it allows us to directly witness, in a seemingly unmediated fashion, the act of wrongdoing. Anything else involves a re-telling of events and fabrication. Thus, we are urged to treat as deeply suspicious those accounts that try to obscure that they are in fact *versions* of events. So, in the world of *The Girl who Kicked the Hornets' Nest*, police detection and official records are of questionable veracity, whilst investigative journalism and autobiography are more trustworthy for clearly indicating their authorship and therefore admitting their partiality. And in failing to recognise the legitimacy of these accounts—not officially sanctioned, not coming from a register of accepted experts, not in a format that resembles evidence—the agents of the state are, again, found wanting.

There are other ways in which Larsson's novel implies that the traditional bases for criminal justice and detection are faulty, most notably in their conception of human behaviour. The modern criminal justice system is founded on an idea of human action as linear and deliberate. As discussed above, the chief concern of this institution is the act of wrong-doing and the moment that directly preceded it in the mind of the perpetrator, the moment of rational decision-making—because, in this model of human behaviour, whether or not a guilty act was *meant* is a defining feature of blame. The detective novel of the early to mid-twentieth century was centrally concerned with human action of this order—with 'whodunnit'. In fact, novels from this period tended to fetishize the rational decision-making process of criminals: in Golden Age detective fiction murder is almost invariably meticulously planned and, more than that, has a clear motive. In Tey's *The Daughter of Time*, too, the search for material evidence to lay bare the act of wrong-doing involves searching for the moment of rational decision-making that preceded it. Inspector Grant frequently suggests that working out the point at which Richard III decided to murder his nephews is crucial to ascertaining his guilt.

One thing that is particularly striking about detective fiction of the late twentieth and early twenty-first century is that it relies far less heavily upon the idea that there is a moment of rational decision-making that precedes a crime. For one thing, a large proportion of murderers in recent detective fiction suffer from psychological disturbances: there is, then, no moment that marks a movement from law-abiding citizen to criminal, no exercise of 'normal' rationality. This is the argument the police detectives make about Lisbeth Salander in *The Girl who Kicked the Hornets' Nest*. The novel suggests that the standard model of criminal action is insufficient overall, and not just in cases of individual insanity: crime, in this novel and the others in the *Millennium Trilogy*, is *never* a discrete event, started at this point *here* and with *this* specific decision. Violence is inevitably carried out by those with childhood experiences of abuse, theft by those inured to an acquisitive culture, intimidation by those with a history of being thwarted. No one chooses to do bad things here, no one thinks through a discrete action, recognises its effect, and deigns to cause harm: they do bad things on impulse, out of habit, and because they don't know better. In this sense, Larsson's novels aren't about 'whodunnit'; blame is far too diffuse, behaviour can't be understood in terms of a linear model of thought-and-then-action, and those who do bad things are rarely presented to us as *agents*, but rather *products* of abusive relationships and cultures of corruption.

All this puts us in mind of Bloch's (1988) astute suggestion that the classic, Golden Age detective novel resembles the process of psychoanalysis (and, he wants to suggest, philosophy) in tracing back to a seminal event that always happened prior to the action that unfolds in the novel. Here's how he describes it:

> Before the first word of the first chapter something happened, but no one knows what, apparently not even the narrator. A dim focal point exists, as yet unrecognised, whither and thither the entire truckload of ensuing events is mobilized – a crime, usually murder, precedes the beginning. ... [T]he reader is absent when the misdeed occurs, a misdeed that, though conveniently home-delivered, shuns the light of day and lingers in the background of the story. It must be brought to light and this process itself is the exclusive theme. (Bloch 1988: 249)

This might chime with fans of, say, Agatha Christie but when we think of post-1970s detective fiction this process of tracing back is, in many cases, less systematic, less likely to end with a satisfying moment of closure (as popular variants of psychoanalysis have it). If the action of the Golden Age detective novel resembles the revelations and redemption of a phobic patient, that of today's detective novel more closely approximates the stabilisation of someone with an organic personality disorder: there is, to put it simply, no primal scene that started it all, no possibility for full recovery. The onus, instead, is on identifying the underlying structures that gave rise to these specific bad episodes.

In post-1970s detective fiction we tend to find social worlds that seem *irreparably* bad—with, it might be added, a detective on the wrong side of the law and with the law on the wrong side of morality. To the crime fiction enthusiast all this may sound very much like what we get in a Raymond Chandler or Dashiell Hammett novel. These hugely successful detective stories of the mid-twentieth century focus on the criminal underworld of US cities and its hold over business leaders, local politicians, and Hollywood stars. The private eyes in these novels—most famously Philip Marlowe and Sam Spade—are inured to a world of corruption that extends to judges and police officers. As Chandler explains in his wonderfully acerbic essay 'The Simple Art of

Murder', the detective of hard-boiled fiction is a cynic when it comes to matters of law enforcement, recognising, as he does, that 'no man can walk down a dark street in safety because law and order are things we talk about but refrain from practicing' (Chandler 1988: 17).

Chandler's sentiment might put us in mind of much twenty-first century detective fiction: here too law appears to be ineffective as an instrument of justice. At the same time, there's much that's unfamiliar to fans of current detective fiction in Chandler's assessment of the achievements of the hard-boiled genre, and that should alert us to the possibility that post-1970s detective fiction is doing something distinctive—and, in turn, that these novels answer to an altogether different popular conception of crime. Take, for example, Chandler's reference to the man walking down a dark street and his imaginary assailant. The image conjured up here is deeply salient in the world of the hard-boiled novel: here victims fall prey to a criminal underworld that commissions brutal and quick killings in the dark recesses of the city. Crime, in twenty-first century detective fiction, is unlikely to involve street violence and more likely to be part of a long-term pattern of abuse and torture, carried out virtually or behind closed doors.

This says something about the difficulty in locating and isolating crime in twenty-first century detective novels. One thing that's particularly striking about this body of literature is that most of the crimes are those for which the material traces and evidence are long gone: we have mainly *historic* cases of domestic violence, child sex abuse, kidnap and enslavement, torture, and assault. Here, horrific abuses stretch back generations. To reinforce this point, Stieg Larsson includes a family tree at the start of his *Millennium Trilogy*. The device is familiar to detective fiction enthusiasts: Agatha Christie, in her first published novel, *The Mysterious Affair at Styles* (1916), includes a map of the home in which the body is found, with an X to mark the place of the corpse. Like Christie, then, Larsson presents us with a familiar diagram of home-life. Unlike Christie, the point is to show that the group to which it refers is rotten throughout, that evil is not isolatable to a single act and individual. We soon realise that this diagram isn't meant as an aid to narrow down suspects and check off the innocence of the rest. It is the *breeding* of hatred, violence, and sadism that is presented to us in this chart, and the long-term, intergenerational abuses that it entails. It's a view of crime that is deeply culturally salient. It is not the corpse on the drawing room carpet that best crystallises our fears about crime today, but the secret, purpose-built torture dungeon.

It's worth pausing here to note another idiosyncratic feature of post-1970s detective fiction. In Chandler and Dashiell's hard-boiled novels, society's power brokers—judges, politicians, business leaders—are frequently implicated in violence. We find this too in twenty-first century detective novels, but here it is social institutions, rather than (simply) individuals in positions of authority, that are bad to the bone. To put it simply, it is less likely to be the private interests of a corrupt judge in the pay of a mobster that threatens social order in twenty-first century detective fiction: it is more usually the principles and conventions that underpin social institutions such as the family, church, criminal law, and the corporation that create the possibility for violence. To return to Stieg Larsson's *The Girl with the Dragon Tattoo*: the distinctive social organisation of the family—its basis in closed, exclusive parent-child relationships and importance to child development—is implicated in, if not partially blamed for the violent episodes in this book.

It's a suggestion we find elsewhere in post-1970s detective fiction. Here, the family is persistently presented as a serious threat to social order because of the problem of learned behaviour and cycles of abuse. And what makes the relationship structures learned in the family all the more criminogenic is the importance placed on maintaining an outward appearance of normality. The result is that harm is concealed and buried in an especially effective manner, so that, those subject to violence become involved in hiding the very sources of harm of which they are a victim. Shame is essential here. It is at once a resource that the family cultivates to encourage its members to conceal experiences that stray from the norm, and, for the wider society, a powerful conditioning force that ensures that the problems of the private realm stay put.

Shame has always been an important feature of detective fiction. It's there in Christie's fiction, as a typical motive for crime. In post-1970s detective fiction, it re-appears in a more complex form. Here, our attention is commonly turned to how shame operates on an everyday basis, how it accumulates, consumes, and disorientates people,[14] as well as its relationship to particular social structures that exist beyond the family. What this fiction offers us, then, is an anatomy of shame. It is no longer simply a dangerous emotional disposition; it speaks of deeper, more long-term and intractable problems. So, for example, much post-1970s detective fiction demonstrates that shame is often attached to sex and sexuality. In the world of the detective novel, this type of shame is taught early-on in the family, and we're asked to see parental—usually paternal—control over this aspect of individual family members' lives as crucial in maintaining control full-stop. And what's most often at risk in the loss of control is the loss of respectability.[15] This means different things, depending on the social context in which a story is set, but most often it's the illusion of a smooth-running family and well-meaning paternalism. One of the achievements of post-1970s detective fiction is the degree to which it resists easy explanations for these ideas about the social order. We're rarely asked to think that it's the family 'what dunnit', or that patriarchal heads of the family are the problem, per se. Instead, the inclination for the family to keep its members in their place, to conceal, to maintain the myth of respectability—and with this, sometimes, to harm, to violate—is linked to such diverse organisations as family-run corporations, civic bodies, schools, local police forces, and religious communities.

The connection drawn between the family, paternalism, and religion—and ingrained patterns of abuse—is a key feature of Åsa Larsson's first novel, *The Savage Altar*, winner of the 2006 award for 'Sweden's Best First Crime Novel'. Here we encounter controlling fathers and unquestioning mothers, charismatic preachers and servile believers—and the problem is as much with the subservient members of these partnerships as the dominant. Set in a remote town in northern Sweden, the story starts with the charismatic young preacher Viktor Strådgard dying on the floor of his church after a vicious knife attack. Viktor's sister, the ethereal Sana, is the prime suspect for his murder. Zealously religious and given to ellipses in memory, Sana seems to be capable of the crime. She's a convenient scapegoat in other respects too; she's a single mother who seems forever on the edge of reason. Sana enlists the help an old friend, Stockholm-based tax lawyer, Rebecka Martinsson, to discover who is responsible for Viktor's death. Through Martinsson—a one-time local disliked intensely by the church elders for kicking up a fuss about being assaulted by one of their number as a teenager—we learn about the community of Kiruna, particularly the centrality of the local church and its influential male pastors. She discovers that the church elders have been fraudulently syphoning off money from the church's charitable trust. And so, the big reveal: one of the church-goers, Curt Bäckström, spontaneously attacked Viktor after walking in on an argument between him and the other pastors about the church's misappropriation of funds. The church elders just stepped back and let it happen.

Larsson, though, doesn't offer us anything further to deduce the levels of responsibility for the murder of Viktor Strandgård. In particular, we're left unsure as to whether the church leaders commissioned the crime or simply failed to intervene. What complicates matters further is that Larsson provides another explanation for Curt's attack. Just before Viktor's death Sana began to suspect that her brother had been sexually abusing her children. She confided in one of the church elders and, finding him relatively uninterested, the doting Curt. Martinsson suggests that Curt may have murdered Viktor to avenge Sana—and, more complicatedly, that Sana told Curt of the abuse with the expectation that he'd confront Viktor. In this explanation of Viktor's murder, Curt walks in on an argument between Viktor and the church elders not about church finances but about the alleged child abuse, and the pastors allow the attack on Viktor because he's become a liability.

Larsson makes it clear that this isn't an *alternative* ending to the story. Rather, she wishes to point out the implausibility of there being a singular explanation for an act of gross violence. In this way, she encourages us to think about the possibility that responsibility might be irreducible to strict lines of cause and effect. In turn, attributing blame might mean producing overly neat, partial stories that exclude the messier aspects of human decision-making and experience. And one element that appears especially difficult to subsume into the officially accepted story of 'whodunnit' in this story and others, is people's moral responsibility to intervene.[16] We find this theme elsewhere in post-1970s detective fiction. It's there, for example, in the first novel in Stieg Larsson's trilogy, a story that closes with Lisbeth Salander angrily pondering Harriet Vanger's responsibility for the ongoing abuse carried out by father and brother, given that she had first-hand experience of that violence, and chose to run away instead of trying to intervene.

Harriet Vanger's failure to intervene is, though, very different to that of the Church elders in Åsa Larsson's *The Savage Altar*, and what distinguishes them, principally, is power. Harriet is a victim of sexual violence, the Church elders highly powerful community leaders. Their moral responsibility to intervene is different in kind. Still, post-1970s detective fiction wants us to think of them as somehow related. For here we tend to find that the inaction of the powerful is one of the soundest tactics for maintaining power and one of the surest ways of compounding harm. And, in turn, the intervention of the powerless—speaking up, detecting, fighting back—tends to be costly and dangerous, partly *because* power so rarely lets itself be seen. Power, in post-1970s detective fiction, means the invisible hand of an unseen boss of a boss of a boss. It means a network of brokers. It means the abusive son of an abusive father, living in a patriarchal society. It means multiple signatories to a bureaucratic process that sanctions violence.

That post-1970s detective fiction nonetheless clearly valorises intervention is really important. We pick this point up again in Chapter 5, where we consider the work literary detectives do to intervene and restore meaning to events. Here, we want to suggest that contemporary detective fiction holds a mirror up to our late capitalist, late modern social world, where the most pressing collective social problems of our age have no clear causes or solutions, no single person or thing to blame, and where, nonetheless, there is an onus on the individual to act. Climate change is perhaps the quintessential example here, where individual interventions matter greatly, but, at the very same time, no single individual or institution is to blame. As the popular slogan has it, 'if you're not part of the solution, you're part of the problem'. Few ideas better illustrate the complicated relationship between responsibility and blame in the twenty-first century. Economic stagnation—that other most pressing collective problem of late capitalist societies—is also something that we know we are implicated in (by, for example, selling over-priced homes, consuming beyond our means), just as, at the very same time, we recognise that blame does not lie at the level of individual action. Our old ideas about responsibility and blame have limited purchase here—the first is too narrow, the second suggests a specific locus. Instead, we're more likely to think that dealing with these problems means asking a more far-reaching and essential question: How should we live? Post-1970s detective fiction also suggests that this is the really important question. We return to this point in the next chapter. For now, we'll simply note that this question directs us to engage in a type of thinking that moves beyond the idea that responsibility and blame come neatly parcelled together. It requires us to think about the structures available or denied to us to live a certain way, collective ideas about the 'good life', and the individual as agentic not just in terms of individual actions, but ethical deliberation.

This is to think about the ways in which post-1970s detective fiction might suggest a way through the problems of late capitalism. This body of literature also, and perhaps more obviously, points out the ongoing, and yet to be reconciled tensions in our culture around blame and responsibility—defining tensions, we would suggest, of late capitalist society. It does so in such a way as to show up the insufficiency of official approaches to detection and truth. Whilst attempts have been made to adapt legal and regulatory frameworks to accommodate new ideas about the diffuse, collective quality of blame—by, for example, recognising joint enterprise, corporate misdeeds, and entrenched, institutional biases—in truth, these frameworks remain best suited to individual misdemeanours and intended actions. It is in post-1970s detective fiction where we find the most eloquent and devastating critique of these traditional, and increasingly outmoded, institutional ideas about crime and justice. This body of literature shows, in rich and fulsome detail, the gap between a modern criminal justice system's approach to matters of truth and virtue and the imagined problem of crime in a recognisably late modern society. The gap might be summarised thus. Modern criminal justice relies upon a conception of crime as a discrete and physical event, preceded by a moment of rational decision-making, and carried out by an individual. It assumes conduct to be traceable, is uncritical about the basis for expert evidence, and (as Lacey, 2012 observes) postpones judgements concerning character. In contrast, the problem of crime, as it is conceived of in so much recent detective fiction, is that it cannot be reduced to a crime scene, a particular event or act, is not part of a linear think-and-then-act process, is rarely the work of a single person, and often implicates a social institution and the culture. This is not to suggest that we have lost a desire for 'heads to roll', but that, increasingly, this is accompanied by a sense that 'the problem' is an endemic one—of the failure of politics (rather than the corrupt politician), the in-built machismo of the financial sector (rather than the rogue trader), and the police as an institution (rather than the bent cop).

In locating the problem of crime in this way, post-1970s detective fiction sketches out a world that is deeply familiar to us—it is one where authority, knowledge, truth, causation, and origin-stories have become in various ways contestable. One of the achievements of this body of literature is that it signals the connections between these contestations and locates them firmly in a social milieu that is distinctively late modern. Sociologists have long suggested that what distinguishes the post-1970s period is the decline of authority and trust, and a new scepticism about truth-claims. These are the familiar features of what we call variously post-modernity, high modernity, the late modern, and the liquid modern. Post-1970s detective fiction asks us to think about what it means to live with uncertainty and distrust, for blame to regularly miss its mark, and for responsibility to seem so difficult to deduce. And it does so, often, by suggesting that the work of detection should be directed towards tracing and catching out power.

In contemporary detective fiction, 'the problem' goes beyond discrete social institutions or groups, but lies in interacting, overlapping structures of power. Åsa Larsson's *The Savage Altar*, for example, implicates the family and religion, but each are underwritten by misogyny and their tendency to allow and hide abuse is exacerbated by the dehumanising effects of late capitalism. None of this can be untangled. None of it *should* be, Larsson seems to suggest: the truth is that we can't really know where the buck stops.

It's a frustrating idea, and one that our culture seems keen to test. Take, for example, the obsessive dramatization of historical events for which the closing act of retribution is a given and the lines of responsibility appear clear. No one doubts that Henry VIII killed Anne Boleyn: that he intended it, and that he was to blame for it. And no one doubts the need for a lengthy compendium of responsible actors involved in the decision to go to war with Iraq, the economic crash of 2008, and the Hillsborough disaster.[17] There are no endings here, in the political intrigues that are the product of our society, and so we return to the ones handed down to us by the age of sovereign power.

The point is that the exercise of power has become less easy to trace, its effects more diffuse, its operation more likely to be self-effacing—and with all that, working out what really happened, who did what (and why), becomes a mysterious, time-consuming affair, the outcomes of which are rarely the fulsome, direct explanations that those seeking justice are after. And so, by way of a final comment, we return to the novel that started this chapter—Karin Fossum's *Calling Out for You*—and the observation that frustrated endings have real effects for people. For Fossum, and so many of today's crime writers the really pertinent question is how it matters to individuals, communities, and institutions that we make someone pay for a loss, in a context where locating the truth of what happened is fraught with problems.

Notes

1. The code of Hammurabi, a legal code produced by the Babylonians of Mesopotamia, is one of the earliest written records of human history, dating back to around 1700 BC. It contains one of the earliest reference to rules around retribution (famously, the idea of an 'eye for an eye'). The Icelandic sagas, as written documents, were produced later—in the thirteenth century—but they also represent important early records of human history in a European context. The sagas detail the feuds between notable Icelandic families, and record how punishments were decided, and settlements reached.

2. There is a significant body of sociological and philosophical literature concerning the idea that we've entered a period of post-modernity, notably (but by no means exclusively) Lyotard (1984, originally 1979), Baudrillard (1994, originally 1981), and Bauman (1992).

3. Most of the British novels of the nineteenth century were originally issued in instalments. Charles Dickens, for example, published most of his novels in serial form, first in Household Words (for which he was

editor), and then in *All the Year Round*, a journal for which he served as both editor and publisher. It was in the latter publication that Wilkie Collins published *The Moonstone* in serial form. Published as a book in 1868, *The Moonstone* is often seen as the first novel-length detective novel. And Edgar Allan Poe—often seen as the earliest detective story-writer on the other side of the Atlantic—used the short story format to write about the exploits of his detective-protagonist, Le Chevalier C. Auguste Dupin.

4. It is the body of literature associated with the sociology of risk where we find the greatest interest in the meaning of responsibility as a distinctively modern concept (see, for example, Baker and Simon 2002; Erikson and Doyle 2003).

5. Take, by way of example, the complex system of rights and legal redress in Ancient Rome, and the way this was organised to protect certain social groups' interests, notably free men of noble birth (see Crook 1976 for an overview, and Gardner 2009 for a discussion of women and roman law). Thus, status was a key feature of all roman legal codes, prescribing, as it did, rights and duties for different groups—and, in turn, different levels of culpability and forms of punishment. And status was not just a matter of being free or enslaved but also being subject to complex rules around guardianship and patronage. Noble-born free-women were in the power of their father, and then husband. Free-born fathers had the right to punish his children, including being allowed to administer death as a penalty. And those slaves that were granted freedom were still beholden to their ex-owners in certain ways. This is a social context where acts mean different things and blame is apportioned according to one's place in a social hierarchy.

6. See Bloch (1988), Brecht (2004), Benjamin (2004) and Frisby's (1992) interpretation of Kracauer.

7. Rabin (2004) explores a set of important changes to English court proceedings in the eighteenth century. Her focus is the various ways in which emotional disclosure came to be side-lined and restricted in the criminal trial because these often-lengthy revelations about a defendant's mental state made determining responsibility difficult. The criminal trial, she points out, became increasingly 'lawyerized', as the perceived need for more tidy explanations of responsibility took hold.

8. The orphaned Oliver, for example, in *Oliver Twist* (1839), is incapable of fully ceding to a life of crime. When we find, towards the end of

the novel, that he comes from a well-to-do family, it's difficult to resist the idea that this was part of the reason why he wasn't fully fitted-out for criminality. Elsewhere, Dickens is clearly interested in the perils of reaching too far beyond the social class one was born into. This is the cause of Pip's undoing, for example, in *Great Expectations* (1861).

9. In a UK context, public trust in the police has been especially well-documented by Reiner (2010). He points to a 'Golden Age' of policing in the mid-twentieth century, where public trust in their work was especially high. This reflects a broader shift in public attitudes. Crozier et al.'s (1975) report 'The Crisis of Democracy' was one of the first to suggest a wholesale decline in trust in democratic government institutions across the global South. Subsequent work has pointed to important variations across countries, and indicated the difficulty in locating trends, but few political scientists would disagree with Crozier et al.'s (1975) central observation, and recent research has suggested a further down-turn in public trust during the twenty-first century (see, for example, IPSOS's Global Trends reports).

10. The British author Nicola Upson has recently published a set of detective novels with an imagined Josephine Tey as the detective-protagonist. They feature Chief Inspector Archie Penrose, a close friend of the real-life Tey, and supposedly the basis for Chief Inspector Grant. One thing that's striking about Upson's novels is that they bring together a style of detection that underpins Tey's novels and distinctively contemporary concerns. *Nine Lessons*, the seventh novel in the series, is a case in point. Here, Tey and Penrose are pursuing a serial rapist—a crime problem that in itself signals that this is a twenty-first century detective novel. The case is solved by Penrose's attention to the material facts of what happened, as much as to Tey's understanding of the place of women in 1930s England, the sort of deep social knowledge that we expect of the twenty-first century literary detective.

11. The idea that most police officers are unable to see the really important clues is an important theme in much nineteenth and twentieth century detective fiction. It's a key feature, for example, of Sherlock Holmes' relationship with Inspector Lestrade, and Hercule Poirot's relationship with Chief Inspector Japp.

12. Much has been written about a general decline in authority in the last quarter of the twentieth century. See, for example, writing on detraditionalization, including Giddens (1990) and Heelas et al. (1995).

13. One of the distinctive features of post-1970s detective fiction is that it allows room for multiple perspectives and narrative voices. Karin Fossum's novels are an especially interesting case in point; here, we're frequently given an insight into the perpetrator's thoughts and feelings. Fossum extends this experiment in The Murder of Harriet Krohn (2015), where the story is told from the murderer's point of view.

14. We're thinking here of novels such as Erik Axl Sund's Crow Girl, first published in English in 2016. Here, we learn that the main protagonist's childhood experiences—specifically, her father's physical abuse—lead to her finding ways of disassociating from the violence and, ultimately, developing multiple personalities.

15. So strong is the desire to maintain the outward appearance of family cohesion and normality that those family members who seriously threaten to reveal abuse are forcibly removed and sequestered. Thus, a recurrent pattern in post-1970s detective fiction is a daughter revealing sexual misadventure or abuse, and then being institutionalised by her parents. This is the case, for example, in Karin Alvtegen's (2003) Missing, where a young woman is institutionalised by her mother after starting a relationship with someone of a lower social class and accidently becoming pregnant. In Stieg Larsson's The Girl Who Played with Fire (2006), Lisbeth Salander is committed to psychiatric care after threatening to reveal her father's violence. And in Erik Axl Sund's Crow Girl, the main protagonist is institutionalised by her father after she gives birth to a child he fathered.

16. The problem of intervention has attracted significant attention elsewhere in our culture, not least of all in the popular idea that late modern societies suffer from a distinctive problem of bystander apathy—that is, the problem of strangers not intervening to protect and support someone in need. This fear, too, arises from a fear that there has somehow been an erosion of individuals' ability or willingness to intervene.

17. The Hillsborough disaster (involving 96 football fans being crushed to death at a stadium in Sheffield, UK) and the Iraq War have both been subjects of extensive, lengthy public enquiries in the UK. The nature of both enquiries tells us much about how responsibility is allocated in the twenty-first century. The Hillsborough Independent Panel published its findings in 2012, twenty-three years after the event. The website detailing the Panel's findings contains 450,000 pages of material. And the

Iraq Enquiry published its findings in 12 volumes in 2016, thirteen years after the invasion of Iraq, and seven years after the enquiry was initiated. Here we have two extraordinarily detailed and lengthy compendia of responsibility, returning complex judgements on what happened long after the events in question.

References

Alvtegen, Karin. 2003. *Missing*. UK: Felony and Mayhem.

Baker, Tom, and Jonathan Simon. 2002. *Embracing Risk: The Changing Culture of Insurance and Responsibility*. Chicago, IL: University of Chicago Press.

Baudrillard, Jean. 1994. *Simulacra and Simulation*. Ann Arbor: University of Michigan Press.

Bauman, Zygmunt. 1992. *Intimations of Postmodernity*. London: Routledge.

Benjamin, Walter, Martin Harvey, and Aaron Kelly. 2004. Travelling with Crime Novels. *The Irish Review* 31 (Spring–Summer): 88–89.

Bloch, Ernst. 1988. A philosophical View of the Detective Novel. *The Utopian Function of Art and Literature*, 245–264. London: MIT Press.

Brecht, Bertolt, Martin Harvey, and Aaron Kelly. 2004. On the Popularity of the Crime Novel. *The Irish Review* 31 (Spring/Summer): 90–95.

Chandler, Raymond. 1988 (originally 1944). The Simple Art of Murder. In *The Simple Art of Murder*, ed. R. Chandler, 1–18. New York: Vintage.

Churchill, David. 2016. Security and Visions of the Criminal: Technology, Professional Criminality and Social Change in Victorian and Edwardian Britain. *British Journal of Criminology* 56 (5): 857–876.

Crook, John A. 1976. *Law and Life of Rome: 90 B.C.–A.D. 212*. Ithaca, NY: Cornell University Press.

Crozier, Michel, Samuel Huntington, and Joji Watanuki. 1975. *The Crisis of Democracy: Report on the Governmentality of the Democracies to the Trilateral Commission*. New York: New York University Press.

Deleuze, Gilles. 2004. The Philosophy of Crime Novels. In *Desert Islands and Other Texts 1953–1974*. Paris: Semiotext(e).

Emsley, Clive. 2005. *Crime and Society in England 1750–1900*, 3rd ed. Harlow, UK: Longman.

Erikson, Richard V., and Aaron Doyle (eds.). 2003. *Risk and Morality*. Toronto: University of Toronto Press.

Foucault, Michel. 1991. *Discipline and Punish: The Birth of the Prison*. London: Penguin.

Frisby, David. 1992. Between the Spheres: Siegfried Krakauer and the Detective Novel. *Theory Culture, Society* 9 (1): 1–22.

Gadda, Carlo Emilio. 1965 (originally 1957). *That Awful Mess on the Via Merulana*, trans. William Weaver. London and New York: NYRB.

Gardner, Jane F. 2009. *Women in Roman Law and Society*. London: Routledge.

Giddens, Anthony. 1990. *The Consequences of Modernity*. Cambridge: Polity Press.

Heelas, Paul, Scott Lash, and Paul Morris (eds.). 1995. *Detraditionalization*. Oxford: Wiley-Blackwell.

Hilliard, Chris. 2017. *The Littlehampton Libels: A Miscarriage of Justice and a Mystery about Words in 1920s England*. Oxford: Oxford University Press.

Lacey, N. 2012. *Women, Crime, and Character: From Moll Flanders to Tess of the D'Urbervilles*. Oxford: Oxford University Press.

Lenman, Bruce, and Geoffrey Parker. 1980. The State, the Community and the Criminal Law in Early Modern Europe. In *Crime and the Law: The Social History of Crime in Western Europe Since 1500*, ed. V.A.C. Gatrell, B. Lenman, and G. Parker. London: Europa Publications.

Lofland, Lyn H. 1973. *A World of Strangers: Order and Action in Urban Public Space*. New York: Basic Books.

Lyotard, Jean-François. 1984 (originally 1979). *The Postmodern Condition: A Report on Knowledge*. Manchester: Manchester University Press.

Rabin, Dana Y. 2004. *Identity, Crime, and Legal Responsibility in Eighteenth Century England*. Basingstoke: Palgrave Macmillan.

Reiner, Robert. 2010. *The Politics of the Police*. Oxford: Oxford University Press.

Sennett, Richard. 1993. *The Fall of Public Man*. London: Faber and Faber.

Sund, Erik Axl. 2016. *The Crow Girl*. London: Penguin.

Tey, Josephine. 1951. *The Daughter of Time*. London: Peter Davies.

4

The Myth of the Good Life

The Myth of the Good Life

The question of 'What is to be Done?' famously asked by Lenin in the context of the politics of pre-revolutionary Russia remains no less topical or relevant. The mantras of 'we have to act now' and its equally expressive 'something should be done' have a constant place in the media, whether to do with the ill treatment of vulnerable individuals, the problems of climate change or the fears of violent disruptions in everyday life. The very technological sophistication and competence of the modern world reinforces the idea that in acting, and choosing to act, we can not only change but also improve the ways in which we live. The steps towards the eradication of disease through both medicine and public health and the establishment of various forms of welfare support were all ways in which it became demonstrably clear that people could act effectively to change negative and dangerous situations. Thus, not acting, and continuing not to act, became an important part of discussions about moral responsibility.

Yet the actual achievements of the second half of the twentieth century in securing relative peace and prosperity for much of the global

© The Author(s) 2019
M. Evans et al., *Detecting the Social*, https://doi.org/10.1007/978-3-319-94520-0_4

north were accompanied by complex implications. That very sense of new found security and a political narrative that, in the words of the Prime Minister Harold Macmillan, suggested that the British people 'had never had it so good', drew attention away from persistent underlying inequalities both at home and in the relationship, both material and cultural, between the global north and the global south. These differences, articulated in the 1960s in terms of the gap between what was then defined as the 'Third World' and more affluent parts of the planet was to become a dominant part of social and political narratives in the latter part of the twentieth century.[1] A new recognition, born out of the struggles for independence on the part of countries once part of the British Empire brought to wider audiences the realisation that the old certainties, in which the goods of those colonies could be claimed by the imperial power, were no longer acceptable. The concept of the 'post-colonial' became a part of political discourse. In this, ideas which were disturbing to many interests were often downplayed by policies of what was called 'development'. But to many in those colonies, 'development' was only the continuation of previous forms of exploitation. As Manuel, an immigrant from Mexico remarks, in Kjell Eriksson's *The Demon of Dakar*:

> Give us a land to live in, he thought, a land where we can toil and love in peace. Why do you have to come to us with your manipulated seeds, your pesticides that give us panting lungs and burning wounds, your agreements that no one can understand until it is too late, fierce police dogs, armed thugs in souped-up jeeps, your drugs and your newspapers and radio stations that only lie?[2]

Eriksson's novel was first published in 2005, by which time many of the aspects of the exploitative relationships between the global north and the global south had been recorded and challenged. But in the 1960s the account of the structural inequalities that resulted from the continuing assumption of colonial power had still to be more widely discussed. It was not that colonial power had not been subjected to critical views. But what remained was a political belief, across much of the west, in the unambiguously positive possibilities of development and progress. With this, as this chapter will discuss, was a highly problematic vision of what constitutes the 'good life', the measure of an endorsed set of expectations about how to live.

Hence when, in 1964, the Labour Party was returned to government it was through an argument about the need for greater 'modernisation' and the more enthusiastic embrace of both technology and a meritocratic social order. The extension of various forms of education (the raising of the school leaving age and the founding of new universities) were part and parcel of this project. But it was not a modernising project which took place against a background of political peace. In the United States the struggle for civil rights and the war in Vietnam produced deadly conflicts, the Fourth French republic had ended in 1958 amid the bitter conflicts of the war in Algeria and in 1968 that country—and other parts of Europe—was to encounter vehement protests by trade unions and students. The idea that post war Europe was to be uniformly peaceful as well as prosperous did not accord with historical reality.

Nor was 'prosperity' uniform. Parts of southern Europe were much less prosperous than the north and all examinations of the internal divisions of Britain, France, Germany or any of the Scandinavian countries quickly established the persistent social and political power integral to the possession of wealth. Although many of these countries saw, in the 1960s, consistently high levels of male employment, the assumption that this would always be the norm began to end in the 1970s, as the price of oil and other raw materials began to impact upon industry. 'Having it so good' was never either universally accepted or experienced; by 1970 the evidence questioning the idea of continuous prosperity had become considerable. But alongside this shift, and in the midst of the various political crises of the 1970s two social changes were taking place which were to have a lasting and fundamental impact upon both Britain and other parts of Europe. One was the change in public attitudes to a wide range of issues connected to sexuality and gender; the other was the shift in the British economy towards a service sector economy and what has become defined as a culture of 'consumption'. If we examine the years between 1970 and 2010 what we see are changes that have transformed many aspects of the lives of all European citizens. The expectations raised in the 1950s (and voiced in Macmillan's remark) did not disappear but they began to take different forms, not least in the ways that a generation born in the years after the end of the Second World War acquired new expectations about consumption.

Participation in various forms of this new 'good life' was founded, as many people found out to their cost in the financial crash of 2008, on increasingly easy access to credit. What can be observed in much of the present global north are parallel changes: greater liberality around issues about gender and sexuality and much less liberality, indeed for many people more constraint, in the terms and conditions of employment. The idea of 'repressive tolerance' which Herbert Marcuse voiced in his essay of 1965 suggested many of these shifts: a world which is less prescriptive towards the intimate lives of its citizens but much harsher in the terms on which individuals are able to support themselves.[3] It is this world which detective fiction in the period after 1970, and with gathering momentum from 1990 onwards, has explored. Not least amongst the ideas that has contributed to this exploration is the articulation of a critical stance towards the apparent virtues of 'progress'. It is a view that was voiced by the critic Walter Benjamin, himself an enthusiastic fan of detective fiction, in an essay of 1940.[4] In one paragraph of the essay entitled *Theses on the Philosophy of History* Benjamin uses the idea of an 'angel of history'. This angel is fully aware of the past and would like to create the present, the place in which he is standing, as a coherent and stable whole. But he is constantly challenged, indeed overwhelmed, by a storm of debris. 'This storm', concludes Benjamin, 'is what we call progress'.

The brief paragraph in Benjamin's essay sets out his horror at the world in which he is writing. In it the combination of technological progress and the necessary passion for change and novelty which is an essential part of the dynamic of capitalism are bringing chaos and destruction to millions of people. The re-building of post 1945 Europe—which Benjamin did not live to see—seemed to offer hope that different forms of 'progress' might emerge. But by the latter part of the twentieth century it had become clear to many people that the appetite for certain kinds of 'progress' was bringing with it danger to both people and the planet. The fierce need for 'growth' was to lead, in 2008, to a financial global crisis which was as significant as that of

1929 had been. The difference between these two events was that the second grew out of the energy of individual material aspirations, and the wish of banks to meet them, even as the loans to support those aspirations could not be maintained through income. But those material aspirations were (and are) an essential part of twenty-first century capitalism; precisely those aspirations that increasingly feed the motivations of characters in detective fiction. But this new form of the 'spirit of capitalism' also gave to it those 'secret quiet men' of whom Rankin had written in *Let it Bleed*. These 'secret' 'quiet' men (in factual terms that gendered term is largely accurate here) who run the corporations and the global financial institutions are not, as is increasingly known, subject to significant political control. For detective fiction this poses—as it did for Inspector Rebus—the new issue of the villains who do not have identities, or at least the difficulty of finding through the myriad details of a corporate structure the 'guilty' party. Moreover, as Michael Lewis made abundantly clear in *The Big Short*, his account of the financing of housing in the USA that triggered the 2008 financial crash, the consequences of the collapse of financial structures are largely experienced by the victims rather than the perpetrators.[5] That tradition within policing which has increasingly demanded retribution for the victim has not, in terms of financial crime been reproduced. Few of those responsible for the mis—selling of finance for housing were ever effectively prosecuted. In much the same way, and in the same decade, the work by the journalist Jill Leovy in her study of the Los Angeles Police Department demonstrates that the deaths of young black men are very seldom investigated: these victims of crime, like those of the victims of unsustainable financial support for housing, cannot assume that those who acted against them will be prosecuted.[6] As Judith Butler, amongst many others, has pointed out, not all lives matter equally.

But the housing crisis in the USA in 2008 was only one instance of the way in which the question of housing, and paying for it, has become critical to the politics and the economics of many western countries This is particularly so in those countries where owning, rather than renting, a place to live is central to general expectations. The narrative about housing in the United Kingdom was transformed by the policy of the government of Margaret Thatcher of the 'right' to buy, a curious amalgam of ideas about the definition of the rights of citizens in terms of the rights to consume.[7] What many people pointed out at the time of the introduction of this policy was that what was being encouraged in the mantra of 'right to buy' was not just the right to buy a house but the specific right to buy council housing, which had been initially financed by general taxation, for general use and not for potential profit. If the same logic or politics had been applied to other forms of socially funded infrastructure, then citizens would presumably have had the right to buy sections of roads or other public buildings. Thus the 'right' to buy, mandatory in a consumer society, was transferred to the individual possession of social resources. The policy of the Thatcher government about housing did not in itself create a new form of entitlement but it was a significant contribution to the idea of the individual ownership of resources created through collective actions. Not least in the importance of this idea is the belief—apparent in global narratives about the way in which progress might be both constituted and assessed—that the accumulation of both the place and the goods of a household space is universally positive. Despite the empirical and global evidence of the physical and emotional evidence of the abusive possibilities of that space, as well as fictional constructions of the dangers of domestic life, it continues to be a potent expression of a 'good life'.[8]

Housing, as everyone who has ever bought or sold a house knows, is a major life event. Many of us have heard, or even taken part in, energetic conversations about the rise and fall of house prices in the UK in the past twenty years. These decades have been a time in which investment in other, more conventional contexts, has become significantly less profitable. The general expectation that has fuelled many of these conversations, and indeed many of the purchases of what is described as buy-to-let has been the assumption that the price of houses will go on rising. This has been the case for much of England, notably the south east of the country. But what is also notable is that in many recent elections, particularly the Parliamentary elections of 2015 and 2017 the places of the greatest success of the Labour Party were the country's large cities, notably London. Part of the reason for this can be explained because of the dramatic rise in the price of housing in London, creating a situation in which the purchase of a house or flat for the majority of the population has become impossibly expensive. The issue has become highly politicised and although the issue is at its most acute in London other cities (for example, Oxford, Cambridge and Bristol) have experienced the same situation. The people living and working in these cities (or others throughout Europe where the cost of housing is also high) have been forced to recognise that in order to work in what has been described as the 'emancipatory' city it is also necessary for that city to provide the infrastructure—which includes housing—that makes this possible.[9] People who live in cities know through the experience of their everyday lives that they need collectively available services and people to service them. The attraction of living in the city is for many the diversity of its service sector and an energetic public space which promises engagement with both the creation and the consumption of immediate forms of culture. For those living in suburbs, on the other hand, it is more likely that the primary concerns are about possible invasions of the social space, especially any new population that might threaten property values and access to privileged schooling. The very diversity that attracts people to the city is less attractive. In these suburbs we can identify the continuity of those forces which Betty Friedan defined in *The Feminine Mystique,* her furious attack on the suburbs of the United States in the 1950s and early 1960s.[10] Central to Friedan's thesis was that these places created ghettos for educated, middle class women, an analysis which now reads as problematic. But these ghettos were not just about the literal loneliness of suburban isolation, they were also about the ways in which an environment praised for factors such as space and general healthiness were actually locations devoid of those local connections essential to the maintenance of social life. Despite critiques such as that by Friedan and new generations of both planners and populations who did not endorse either the spatial or the social aspects of suburban life it was nevertheless a blueprint for domestic life that has continued.

It is this fracture, the distance between the fantasy of the 'good life' which a home in the suburbs will provide and the reality of that experience which is central to one of the most pertinent detective novels of the twenty-first century: Tana French's *Broken Harbour,* first published in 2012.[11] The novel concerns housing in the Republic of Ireland, a country which was to experience its own rapid boom in the price of houses and then an equally fast collapse. Georg Simmel wrote in 1907 about the 'speed' at which money can operate and through which we assume that we can immediately transform our lives.[12] But he could not have predicted the hysterical urgency of an estate agent, whether real or fictional, urging a client in the twenty-first century that 'the market is moving really fast' and that a purchase, advisable or not, should be made immediately. It was just such a fictional estate agent who, in *Broken Harbour*, persuaded the Spain family to buy their new house in the suburban hinterland of Dublin. The house was described in advertisements as 'A new revelation in premier living. Luxury house and apartments now viewing'. The Spain family, husband, wife and two children are entranced by this vision. They are all reassured that the chaos of abandoned building materials and the desert like silence of the surrounding area will soon be 'landscaped' to that mythical 'high quality' so beloved by the writers of the advertising material about housing.

What Tana French does is *Broken Harbour* is to bring together two narratives that have formed, and still form, seductive visions of life in the twenty-first century west. The first is that of living in a settled family unit, secure in the sense of a relationship sanctioned by some form of state or religious ceremony and one in which the parties, notably the adults, have consensual attitudes to their roles and their responsibilities. In this case the family at the centre of the novel follows that pattern of a man who is the major earner, a wife taking care of children and home. It is of course a pattern that has become increasingly rare as economic pressures make it increasingly unlikely that any household, with or without children, can be supported on the income of one person. But this family is committed to that model, and as far as readers can detect at the beginning of the novel, entirely happy with it. Despite the evidence of a range of both non-fiction and fiction from the 1950s onwards which suggests that this form of conventional life in the suburbs makes people, especially female people, very unhappy if not clinically depressed, the presentation of a way of life in which the purchase of a home outside central urban areas is linked to an idea of the good life still continues.

Unhappily for the Spain family their new home very rapidly becomes anything but that ideal environment for family life that they had envisaged. The walls of the house are found to be less than substantial, the husband loses his job, the detritus of the building work is not cleared, and the jobless husband becomes convinced that some alien force, either human or animal, is living in the house. In the search for this creature he begins to drill into the fragile walls but finds nothing. As the family continues to try and continue its everyday life and its accompanying social relations the cracks that continue to appear in their existence are personal as well as material. Life in the increasingly value-less house gets worse and worse. The Spain family is caught in that nightmare of every property owner of 'negative equity'; the house is now worth far less than they paid for it but the debt for the loan remains the same. In these unhappy circumstances a terrible event occurs at the Spain household. One day the husband and the two children are found murdered, the wife severely injured. Here there has to be a 'spoiler alert'. Although the police pursue various leads, notably the conventional but entirely empirically unlikely idea, that an unknown assailant has entered the house and killed three of its inhabitants it eventually emerges that it is the mother who is the killer. Driven to distraction by the collapse of her dream world the only way out she can see is that of destruction. The perfect house no longer exists and so, it would seem, neither can the perfect family.

The end of the dreams of the Spain family are exactly those of the thousands of people across Europe and the United States who have seen either the value of their house collapse or who have no choice except to default on their mortgage repayments. As has been widely acknowledged, the economic crisis of 2008 was in large part created out of the accumulated bad debts of the housing markets of the United States. Thousands of people did not have the money to sustain their fantasies. But the fantasies did not disappear from either individual or collective forms of consciousness. Property advertisements continue to construct the kind of desirable, urban life style that can be achieved through the purchase of the 'right' kind of property. Individuals talk with enthusiasm of 'getting on the property ladder', without interrogating the idea that an initial purchase of property inevitably constitutes some form of immensely desirable and inevitable progression towards better and better forms of housing and apparently, of life. Property, in this language, becomes a career.

What has been set up through this particular set of aspirations is, for the majority of individuals, new possibilities of insecurity and concern. Insecurity takes the form of concern about the maintenance of the value of a property (part of the Spain's emerging nightmare is that their heavily mortgaged house keeps losing its value) and an endless fear that the employment which supports the payments for property will disappear. The concepts of 'precariousness' and the world of the 'precariat' have become part and parcel of the vocabulary of social scientists but their associative reach can arguably be extended to many categories of people outside the usual definition. Hence it is not only those on zero-hour contracts or seasonal work who live 'precarious' lives; it is those many in apparently more secure employment who nevertheless live lives dominated by the fear of financial loss. Loss which is not in this case about the loss of life or of significant others but of income and the value of the property to which that income is committed.

It is this new seam of collective insecurity which detective fiction in the period after 1970 so forcefully investigates. Characters, particularly those who become murderous, have always had fears in detective fiction: generally, those fears are about some disclosure of their misdeeds or the loss of actual or potential wealth. But the form of fear in the past fifty years which detective fiction has identified is that of collective fear: the experience in the late twentieth and early twenty-first century of living in a world which offers the paradox of increasingly vast—and demonstrated and universally visible—private wealth in a context where collective forms of security are disappearing or being abolished. What has been identified as the 'politics of fear' has often been suggested as a form of cultural politics, a politics which creates fears about, for example, the safety of children.[13] But it is suggested here is that there is a much more general and intrusive fear at work in much of the global north: fears which are generated from material concerns.

Where this takes us in terms of detective fiction is to two themes: one the extent to which individuals (such as the character of JW discussed in Chapter 2) who are determined to make as much money as possible. The other is the extent to which 'money' itself has become an increasingly complex subject. Money, as Scott Fitzgerald memorably remarked, 'talks'. What demands investigation here is the way in which detective fiction has recognised the ways in which what economists describe as 'financialization' has transformed aspects of lives. The term in its most specific sense refers to the increase in the importance and the influence of the financial sector. That 'influence' is multi-dimensional; it relates to political influence as well as the influence over individual lives. Thomas Piketty's *Capital* is one of the many works which has explored the origins and consequences of the shift in capitalist economies from an economy which is primarily dependent on manufacturing for the making of profit to an economy which is dependent on the manipulation of the workings of the financial sector. The growing gap between rich and poor, the social inequality which has come to attention across the political spectrum, is the result, Piketty argues, of the growth in highly concentrated forms of the making and the manipulation of money. In a novel by John Lanchester, also with the title *Capital*, we see the working out of this new economic system. The Yount family at the centre of Lanchester's novel, whilst rather better off than the Spain family, is also heavily invested in property. The 'good life' in Lanchester's novel is a more expensive and metropolitan one than that of the Spains but it still depends on the assumption that two forms of wealth will always increase: one is that of property and the other is that of the rewards of the financial sector. Both families are dependent on high levels of risk and specifically the risk of taking on considerable personal debt in order to finance the houses which they hope will vastly increase in value. As John Lanchester has pointed out, people who live in desirable houses in equally desirable parts of the London district of Clapham often live in houses which are worth 100 times median annual income.[14] Owning one of these houses depends either (or both) on significant amounts of inherited wealth or much higher than average earnings. The Yount family does not come to such a disastrous end as that of members of the Spain family. But what is made transparently clear in the novel is the same narrow and indeed precarious line between a degree of solvency and a collapse into debt.

In the novels by both French and Lanchester one aspect of the 'good life' deserves mention. It is the strength of the relationship between women and various aspects of property. This does not simply take the form of literal concern about ownership of property, but it is about the making and the beautification of the home. Both wives, in French and Lanchester, invest considerable time and money in bringing their homes to what they perceive as desirable standards. Re-decoration is a constant theme as is attention, as any glance at media advertisements about the home and housing will demonstrate, to changing fashions for the home. This is not about fashion for the individual self but for the kitchen or the bathroom or the paint colour of the walls. All these aspects of the interior of the home are invested with huge amounts of social and symbolic capital: the Spains do not aspire to the same standards as the Younts but Mrs. Spain is similarly aware of the meanings and values that are attached to the interior decoration of her home. As creatures living in these much-valued homes both Mrs. Yount and Mrs. Spain are as aware of their own appearance as they are of their homes: not only must the home reflect the person, but that person must reflect the home. The expensively decorated interior space of the home merits a person who can replicate that same careful attention to visual changes. Social historians have long remarked on the household as an inevitable site of consumption. To which we can add the intensification of that consumption through the making of the home as a further location for that exercise of the restless and always changing demands of fashion. Resistance to consumerist domestic ideals may, however, be possible and fictional detectives are often vocal dissenters.

A considerable body of detective fiction, in the presentation of the domestic space of many male policemen cuts across this narrative of the thirst for home ownership and the beautification of the domestic space. In doing so, it implicitly (and in some cases explicitly) rejects the values that make up the home owning ideal. For certain policemen, and Rankin's John Rebus is an exemplary example of this phenomenon, the ideal of a settled domestic life is tantamount to imprisonment. (In the Rebus novels his encounters with domestic life range from the accidental death of the cat belonging to his one-time lover Patience to acute physical and mental indigestion spent with a colleague set on parading the joys of domestic life).[15] We might set against this the tradition in which George Simenon's Inspector Maigret not only returns at a regular time every evening but also goes home for lunch. Ruth Rendell's Chief Inspector Wexford, in a later generation, is similarly blessed with an immaculately ordered home and of course there was never a Golden Age detective more concerned not only with domestic order but precise domestic order than Christie's Poirot. However, the domestic conditions in which male detectives live lives verging towards the minimal, if not the squalid, end of the continuum could be read as an entirely accurate assessment of the consequences of the absence of the time, energy or financial resources to invest in domestic space. Statistical information from various countries about the personal lives of those working in the police suggests that it is a profession in which rates of divorce are high. In that context what detective fiction is the reality of real life detectives. But another way of reading the manifest disinterest in domestic comfort that is common (although not universal) in detective fiction is that what writers are doing is implicitly presenting a form of resistance to precisely those ideals and those imperatives which have come to constitute so much of the western ideal of the 'good life'. At the same time there remains considerable cultural attraction in the ancient figure of the lonely hunter for truth and justice. The contemporary construction of the demands of the 'good life' may not facilitate this way of life. For centuries the decoration, care and equipment of a domestic space has been assumed to be the responsibility of women. 'Making a good home' being, as historians of domestic life have demonstrated, something usually done by women through the resources which men provide.

The famous gendered division of domestic labour which has attracted so much attention since the 1970s does, however, pose questions for writers of detective fiction. Given that domestic skills are—still—assumed to be largely the realm of women, to portray male detectives with concern about their homes might suggest a degree of association with domestic affairs suggestive of a sexual ambiguity which could complicate the presentation of male characters. As this is written, there are very few either gay or transgender people in the police forces of detective fiction across Europe; the pursuit of crime would appear to have remained resolutely heterosexual. However, this apparent endorsement of sexual uniformity should not be taken as an indication of the way in which masculinity is presented by writers of detective fiction. What emerges from reading the detective fiction of the past fifty years is that although the happily married or about to be married heterosexual policeman with a well-ordered home is rare, what is not rare is the way in which numerous authors, across Europe, create detectives who, whilst heterosexual, nevertheless resist many of the more conventional expectations of masculinity. Detective fiction, in short, does much to problematise masculinity. It does so in three ways: the presentation and condemnation of both physical and emotional violence in the culture of the police, the recognition of 'outsider' intelligence and the search for bodily, feminised, comforts by central characters. In doing this what detective fiction has often implicitly suggested is that the ideals of the domestic 'good life', of care and courtesy towards others, should also be displayed at work. Bridging the gap between the domestic and public versions of the 'good life' has been part of the 'civilising mission' (to use the words of the sociologist Norbert Elias) of some writers of detective fiction.

The culture of the work of policing has long been presented as one in which male violence, both physical and verbal, is an accepted part. Moreover, that violence applies as much to the police as to those pursued. In police forces which until very recently have found it difficult to integrate either women or racial and sexual minorities the professional 'space' for the existence of different views about the use and tolerance of physical violence has not been extensive. As non-fiction literature has demonstrated both racism and sexism have existed, and exist, to an often extraordinary degree. So, in fiction a problem exists for writers who wish to create a positive male figure; gentlemen amateurs are no longer viable as characters in the twenty-first century and professional detectives have to work in institutional worlds replete with problematic habits and values. Solutions to this question include writers who create male detectives who either inhabit the chronological past—and who then stand as forces of possibly progressive values—or who operate in some kind of tangential place of policing. In the first instance the writing of William Shaw stands out, in that his series of Breen and Tozer novels is set in the UK in the 1960s, that decade symptomatic of the possibilities of social and cultural change, not least around questions of sexuality.

The male central character of Shaw's novels is not in Sergeant Cathal Breen, the son of an immigrant Irish builder. Hence a central character whose father was a member of a national group that was often refused access to the 'good life' either, or both, through lack of access to housing or employment. But Breen has arrived in the London police force and in the series of novels that accompanies Breen and his eventual partner Helen Tozer they make their joint way through the world of the sexist attitudes and actions of their colleagues. Breen is an outsider through his national origins; equally so through his disinclination towards taking part in the drinking and casual sexual encounters of his colleagues. Throughout the series of novels Breen's views, habits and values are contrasted with two distinctly different sets of ideas: one that of an older generation and the other that of the changing culture of London in the 'swinging' sixties. In the first of the novels (*A Song from Dead Lips*, first published in 2013) Helen Tozer's arrival as a trainee detective is created with incredulity by Breen's colleagues. At that point in the history of English policing women were not expected either to be detectives or to drive police cars; views reflected in Breen's office:

> "What?" said Carmichael, "we've got to work with a bloody plonk?"[16]

Nor is female solidarity much in evidence. The office secretary Marilyn is no supporter of Helen Tozer:

> [Breen] was making a note of the conversation in his notebook when Marilyn passed close to his desk and whispered, "Only saying. She's on the pill. It's common knowledge, you know what that means."
> "What?"
> "Helen Tozer. She's a S-L-A-G"
> Marilyn raised her eyebrows meaningfully and then turned her back.[17]

Marilyn's negative attitude towards Tozer continues into the second volume of the series. When one of the detectives uses the phrase 'free love' about a household of young people Marilyn turns to Tozer and sneers, 'I expect you'd like that. Free love.'[18]

Breen and Tozer eventually become not just colleagues but also lovers and parents. But in doing this they present themselves, and are presented by William Shaw, as two people attempting to reconcile competing norms about sexuality. 'Old' sexism, the 'laddish' culture of the police station is contrasted with the young women (including Helen Tozer) whom Breen meets in the course of his job and through the inescapable reality of living in a London being transformed by new forms of music and dress. But what is also central to all the Breen and Tozer novels is the examination of the past through this fiction and the way in which Shaw positions Breen as central to a discussion of how—and if—masculinity has changed since the late 1960s. In portraying the language, and attitudes to women and gay people, in ways that would now be regarded by many people as entirely unacceptable, Shaw is also asking us to consider how and to what extent that culture has changed. For example, Tozer, again in *A Song from Dead Lips*, is asked as a matter of course to make the tea for her colleagues.[19] But before we exclaim at this instance of a sexist past we might recall a young office worker in London of 2016 who was required to wear high heeled shoes as part of her job. Sexism, Shaw is asking us to consider, can take many forms.

Both the language and sexist attitudes of men in the English police force of the 1960s come under critical scrutiny in Shaw's novels. But so too do two other areas where the culture associated with masculinity is explicitly questioned by Breen. The first is the physical violence of the police and the second is its institutional corruption. Before the various Acts of Parliament which re-wrote the ways in which suspects could be questioned, the idea that those assumed to be guilty could be forced to confess through various forms of duress was, as significant real-life cases demonstrated, all too common. When confronted by such acts Breen becomes the voice of refusal of these practices. Here he is offered a cricket bat in order to threaten and coerce a suspect:

> "We saved his legs for you", said Carmichael, holding up a cricket bat… Don't hit him too hard. Just a bit of fun'.[20]

In Shaw's *A House of Knives* a secretary says '…everyone knows we rough people up a bit. Its only to be expected'.[21] These, and other instances of 'bits of fun', are scattered throughout Shaw's novels.

These, and other instances stand, not just as background to a novel, but as a testament to an actual police culture which resulted in such widely reported miscarriages of justice as those known as the Guildford Four and the Birmingham Six. Less well known were the cluster of cases associated with DS Derek Ridgewell in the 1970s. These cases (the Oval Four, the Stockwell Six and others) all involved false accusations against young black men. In these cases, the judgments were overthrown and Ridgewell was imprisoned. But what remained, as the policing of the case of the murder of the black teenager Stephen Lawrence in 1993 even more dramatically demonstrated, was both the institutional racism of policing and the intense pressure on the police to bring successful prosecutions. There is no reason to assume that the latter pressure has changed, albeit in different manifestations. The police, judged through the league tables that accompany their work, remain anxious for successful prosecutions. In all these real and factual cases what is occurring is physical force between men, and men—as Shaw makes clear—who are prepared to use that strength to assert their dominance.

The use of violent means to secure confessions and hence convictions is in itself a form of corruption. But another more literal form of corruption which Shaw explores is that of financial bribery. Here Breen listens to the pitiful lament of a colleague involved in an illicit money-making scheme:

> I'm not one of those coppers…And then I met these CID guys from Peckham who were running a coat-hanger scheme, selling keys to gangs and taking their bit and they were making a fair whack of money. And the shopkeepers were all insured, so where's the harm? And they showed me how easy it was.[22]

The justification of this particular policeman for taking part in this scam is that it is the only way that he can support his wife and a sick child. But the point of Shaw's narrative is surely to counter assumptions about the absolute honesty of the police and to suggest that not only is Breen determined to bring to justice those who kill and injure but is equally determined to do it in acceptable ways. The result, the conviction, is not the only point of Shaw's narrative. The means and the process of detection are also central to the making of justice and, implicitly, the 'good' society.

In the 1960s, as remains the case in the second decade of the twenty-first century it is men and the masculine who are largely charged with policing and with ensuring that way of life which families such as the Spains wish to enjoy. But Shaw, and others, are also exploring the location and the origins of the intelligence necessary to police effectively. This, as virtually all authors of detective fiction stress, is not merely a question of educational qualifications. Higher education is not widely endorsed in detective fiction. But what is endorsed is an intelligence and an awareness of others that might be named 'outsider' intelligence. This form of understanding of the world is significantly not associated with conventional forms of masculine success: the handsome, the academically brilliant, the outstanding sportsman, all forms of conventional and largely heterosexual masculinity do not appear in large numbers in detective fiction. Indeed, the widely acclaimed French writer of both crime and mainstream fiction, Pierre LeMaitre has created a detective who is exceptionally small in stature, has no interest in masculine sports or hobbies but is exceptionally competent at his job.[23] This form of the crossing of lines, the blurring of conventional expectations is everywhere in detective fiction. Shaw's Breen is typical of this consistent form of anti-hero, sharing with his dead father any easy assumption of national or sexual characteristics:

> At home, Breen's father had been quietly dismissive of the Irishmen he worked with. They arrived by the boatload, desperate and uneducated, carrying dreams of sending fortunes home. Many of the gangers treated them badly, keeping them in beer but paying them a pittance. The English hated them and put up cards in their windows. No Blacks. No Irish. 'Ignorant Bogtrotters' his father called them, but Breen never knew whether this was a warning to avoid manual labour.[24]

This father's relationship to his own national origins could be read as a form of self-hatred but Shaw is careful to make it clear that Breen's father is attempting to articulate something more complex. It is a striving for values that are not conventionally derived. As a man who fled to England with the pregnant wife of another man, Breen's father had much to escape from in terms of the coercive religious authority of the Irish Republic in the 1950s. Breen himself knew little of this story until after this father's death. But the knowledge of that history gives to Breen a sense that the conventional order is not necessarily justifiable, let alone compassionate or tolerant.

Male violence, William Shaw makes clear in all his Breen and Tozer novels, is *learned* violence. Moreover, much as that violence is often learned through patterns of domestic violence it is also learned through the enforced violence of those historically largely male institutions of the military and the police. The language of legitimation of those institutions has also been (and remains) one of force: 'crushing', 'destroying', 'stamping out' and other similar expressions are examples of police comments. In the third Breen and Tozer novel, *A Book of Scars*, the plot is informed by the suggestion that the violence learned and taught to British troops during the British campaign against the Mau Mau in Kenya in the 1950s became part of the personal history of the men serving in forces at that time. It was carried into their behaviour in the years long after the cessation of those conflicts. The evidence in the UK about the levels of mental illness in the men who have served in armed combat suggests that professionally instilled and organised violence is seldom left on the battlefield.

In the character of Breen, Shaw is presenting us with a man who stands apart from those politics of 'law and order' in which it is thought that the only way to secure social peace and security is through harsh forms of punishment. It is, Shaw is also suggesting, a form of social illiteracy to suppose that violence against persons is not associated with both personal and social history. Since it is—empirically and in fiction—largely men who inflict physical violence on others, for men not to react to this with other forms of violence requires, as Breen and scores of other writers of detective fiction writing after 1970 recognise, often very difficult. The novels of—to mention only a few—John

Harvey, Matthew Frank, Yrsa Sigurðardóttir, David Mark, Anne Holt, Arnaldur Indriðason and Val McDermid, all point to the long-term consequences of physical abuse. These abusive acts may be both domestic or derived from state policies. Whatever the origins these are acts from which neither those who inflict the violence or receive it ever fully recover: the title *The Book of Scars* might be said to be applicable to significant numbers of crime novels. Amongst those novels is Matthew Frank's *If I Should Die* in which an ex-soldier, living rough speaks of the psychic consequences of being a professional soldier:

> Did you know that on average, a male veteran suffering PTSD symptoms will not seek help for fourteen years? So instead of appearing on military statistics they get chalked up later as mental health issues, domestic violence, alcohol and drug abuse, unemployment, homelessness, suicide… War's just a video game now… hardly anyone gets hurt any more, do they?[25]

This comment takes us into the world of Jean Baudrillard and his work on the fantasies which we entertain about the reality of the deployment of state power.[26] But it is also an element in the way in which recent detective fiction has come to articulate the social impact and meaning of the idea of a culture of violence. Not just a culture which belongs to, or is lived in by criminals, but a culture which informs everyday language and behaviour. In this culture what detective fiction does with great consistence is to demonstrate that although men are violent towards each other it is often women who are the victims of male violence. The novels by Jo Nesbø frequently revolve around physical danger to women; the men who control women through various forms of violence are as constant and as present in detective fiction as they are in fact.

The men who are responsible for policing this culture and who appear as the central characters in the crime fiction of Europe in the decades after 1970 are, in large part, well aware of the complexity of the boundaries of violence and its presence as both online entertainment and actual physical assault on others. What comes with this is a growing concern, epitomised by Breen but shared by other fictional characters, about maintaining intimate relations conducted with an *absence* of violence. For these characters there is no easily available template for the 'good man', and certainly very little time or energy for maintaining that stable domestic life which is constitutive of the 'good' life. The characters in the novels of William Shaw, John Harvey and David Mark (again to mention only a few) do not fit easily into those general categories of 'good chap' or even the basically 'sound' but slightly flawed (by drink or whatever else) characters of the period up to and including the 1970s. What all these male characters have (at least for some of the time) is a settled and supportive domestic life. On the other hand, an overwhelming characteristic of the male characters is that of individuals without many of those secure anchors—of partners, homes—which were once if not universal then at least more common in detective fiction. To be a policeman, to be the very individual who is given the responsibility for patrolling the 'good life', comes with the cost of being at some distance from participation in it. Even if a fictional detective is given a loving, and permanent relationship—as is the case for David Mark's central character Aector McAvoy—that person comes from outside conventional society. McAvoy's wife Roisin is from a traveller community, exactly the kind of community and way of life which many within the conventional world, and the world of Mark's novels, regard as entirely hostile to all that they stand for.[27] Social boundaries, in this fiction, are far from disappearing. The classic separations of class, gender and race remain consistent. But more literal social boundaries, that a 'nice' home means security and happiness, are becoming more suspect. Perhaps most important of all is that the 'new' detectives have highly sceptical views about the world which they are tasked with defending.

This suspicion of the very definition and purpose of their employment comes with the continuity of a longstanding tradition within detective fiction in which senior officers and those in positions of institutional power are often incompetent or corrupt or both. These senior figures may be genial (Inspector Morse has some affection for his commanding, not very bright, officer) but they do not match the intelligence and the perception of their more junior staff. An aspect of this with a powerful relationship to questions of the 'good life' is that these senior figures are often deeply imbued with financial social or domestic ambitions. They want large houses, comfortable ways of life and recognition in local and national networks. Perhaps few reach the heights of absurdity of Superintendent Mullett, the commanding officer of R.D. Wingfield's Inspector Jack Frost series, but many follow the same path. In this vein of detective fiction lies a continuity between mainstream and crime fiction: from the days of Jane Austen and George Eliot the assumption of virtue of those in social hierarchies has been consistently challenged.

But the costs of the achievement of the good life which seniority in a career structure may bring are seen as considerable by the majority of writers of detective fiction. There is little acceptance of the idea that there is such a thing as a 'good life' and that it is possible to achieve it by adherence to a set of conventional norms. Upsetting the 'good life' comes in a number of ways, of which crime is one. But it can also come in fictional narratives about the actual detection of crime. Thus although fictional detectives are seldom social or sexual radicals, their distance from mainstream convention is sufficient for them to to stand collectively as a critical voice about the 'good life'. Most marked, perhaps, is the lack of interest voiced by most fictional detectives in making or acquiring money. Indeed, for many detectives there are problems about managing on their pay. Mankell's Wallender is always worrying about money, as is the female detective in Erik Axl Sund's *The Crow Girl*, Detective Superintendent Jeanette Kihlberg.[28] It is not that detectives in any western police force are any more badly paid than any other public-sector worker but that the demands and the nature of their work involves costs (of eating out, of working in dirty conditions) that are absorbed by the individual rather than the employer. The way of life of a fictional detective, in pursuit of a criminal and awake at all hours, is not one which makes for careful budgeting. But across European versions of noir the commitment to making money is generally regarded as suspicious; the critical expression of 'being on the make' is one that sits uneasily with what has become endorsed as the inherent value of 'entrepreneurship', a virtue increasingly expected in many contexts outside that of financial markets. It is striking, across detective fiction, that it is both those who commit crime successfully and those who are most promoted in the pursuit of criminals who inhabit the large houses and drive the expensive cars. The material situation of the pursued and the pursuers is very often similar. This raises the question of various forms of moral collusion, and, not least, the close examination of the ways large amounts of money are made.

If this lack of interest in making money separates fictional detectives from both the 'real' world and their imagined superiors, there remains one final example of social distance between fictional detectives and the world they are charged with defending: namely that of their own abuse of their own bodies. Inspector Maigret, as noted, went home to lunch. Nobody, at the time of the novels' publication remarked on this habit. Now there are probably very few people in the western world whose days are marked by regular meal times and strict demarcations between meals. The world of detection, in both fact and fiction, has always had to operate round the clock but it is clear that in the twenty-first century the hours of policing have increased not just in length but in terms of their irregularity. It is simply taken for granted by authors of detective fiction that characters will work day and night. Inspector Rebus is just one of the many fictional detectives whose personal life has been wrecked by appointments not met and promises not kept. There is always another drink to be had, another lead to be pursued. These habits, of what Rebus comes to see as the neglect of both his marriage and his role as a father are not, however, always necessarily judged as severely in the case of a man as they are for a woman. It is perhaps for this reason that the impossibility of living a 'good life' for women detectives is seldom fully explored. Being single, certainly without children, would seem to be mandatory for a woman detective. David Mark's character Detective Superintendent Trish Pharaoh stands out here: a single parent with children, she is presented as a direct contrast to the domestic virtues of Roisin McAvoy, even as her very eccentricity is presented as part of her shield against the world. The neglect by a male parent of a child might be forgiven, by a woman it would be unacceptable. Such are the difficulties for women of living the life conventionally expected of women (the management of a home, the care of others) that it is perhaps not surprising that twenty-first century detective fiction more often creates male characters than female ones. There are now women in fictional police forces (Eva Dolan's Detective Sergeant

Ferreira or Lisa Cutts' Detective Constable Nina Foster for example) but what is interesting is that their emotional fragility is exactly that: it is not a vulnerability which is expressed through drug or alcohol use.[29]

That flagrant self-abuse of many detectives is yet another, and here the final, instance of the ways in which fictional detectives flout the expectations of not just the 'good life' itself but also of the expectations of how to live such a life. The diet of many fictional detectives is loaded with all those items which we are warned are, if not actually toxic, then at least hostile to our general well-being. Fats, fast food, drugs, sugar, alcohol and cigarettes are all consumed in large quantities, contrary to both medical advice and the laws of various countries. Given the attention devoted to the appearance of the body, not least in terms of its size and shape, in the twenty-first century west, fictional detectives stand out as serial dissenters from this pre-occupation. There are of course that distinctive minority of those equally fictional male detectives who are competent and interested cooks: John Harvey's Inspector Resnick enjoys cooking and is happy to instruct his female companions in its possibilities. Breen has similar interests. But what unites these characters with those detectives less interested in culinary joys is that neither group has any voiced interest in their overall appearance. All notice that they are sometimes looking old, grubby or dishevelled but there is little personal narcissism amongst fictional detectives of any gender. This group of people does not stand in front of mirrors, either real or imaginary, and worry about their dress and overall demeanour. If we contrast this with the interests of another contemporary genre of fiction, that of what are described as 'shopping and fucking' novels then the gap is considerable. Nobody wears labels, in the sense of identifiable brands of clothes; we are never told about the possible delights of the finest fabrics or the most exotic clothes. Men, in these novels, do what heterosexual men have traditionally supposed to do: have little or no interest in clothes. This may be marker of a very conventional aspect of crime fiction; but we might also view it as a form of dissent in a culture which is laden with the objects and aspirations of consumption as constitutive of the 'good life'.

One final comment here on the question of dissent and dissenting in the contemporary detective novel. European crime novelists of the past five decades have observed, with an accelerating focus, various forms of social change that have been brought about through national and international politics. Amongst these forms of social change and one which demands emphasis is the increasing legitimization of various forms of competition. This takes the form of repeated political calls for all adults (largely regardless of their personal responsibilities) to be economically active but it has also involved the introduction of various forms of measurement in many professional locations. In universities and schools across Europe this has taken the form of 'league tables'; in health and social services 'targets' have accompanied 'efficiency gains' to introduce new demands into those contexts. No police force, and no police force in fiction, has escaped these new forms of bureaucracy. It is impossible for any individual, in any form of paid work, to escape from the assumption that to compete is an innate human characteristic. Constraints on what Thomas Hobbes described in the seventeenth century as the 'war of all against all' are often rare in circumstances of material need. Those circumstances, in the late twentieth and early twenty-first century are not circumstances in which populations in the west are threatened by famine or epidemic disease. But we are threatened by the prospect of 'not succeeding', of what the journalist Barbara Ehrenreich described in 1989 as the middle class 'fear of falling'.[30] How to exist in this increasingly generalised culture of not achieving the 'good life' can be seen in various responses of detective fiction.

The first is that of the validation of the talented, but anarchic outsider, who challenges the regime of personal conformity. Jo Nesbø's Harry Hole is no conformist and as such is difficult for the Norwegian police force to corral him successfully. His time sheets and case notes are not in perfect order. But he has two characteristics which enable him to escape from professional competition: he is strikingly successful in his pursuit of criminals and as such the very culture which so enthusiastically endorses success has to tolerate his less than perfect compliance with bureaucratic standards. The second characteristic is that Hole has no interest in material rewards: he does not want in the ways which convention demands.

But 'wanting', for both real and fictional characters, does not always take material form. It may also be about access to other forms of privilege. In William Shaw's *The Birdwatcher* the man eventually revealed as the villain of the piece is the man who is so engaged in ambitions of social mobility that he has engaged a private tutor to ensure that his son will be accepted by the University of Cambridge. In one sense this is a contemporary, factual, example of the energy and money that sections of the British middle class have put into ensuring a privileged and privileging education for their children. But what it results in, in the final pages of the novel, is a young man killing his father. The son has realised that he does not wish to occupy the social space that his father wishes to provide for him. It is not just the individual sins of the fathers that are recognised by their children but so is the world which those fathers have attempted to create.

The 'good life' which the Spains and millions of other people across Europe have hoped for, and continue to hope for, has become increasingly fragile in the world of the twenty-first century. Not everyone, fortunately, lives in an increasingly valueless, collapsing, house. Very few people kill their children. These dramatic incidents in fictional narratives are seldom part of real life. But the content and the structure of the dreams that inspire these events are very real and are seldom contested in coherent and effective ways. On the contrary, political narratives often speak for the continuation and protection of that 'good life' which is so hard to both achieve and maintain. Despite those increasing numbers of critics who have spoken of the cost both to the people of the global south and the planet as a whole of the western version of the 'good life' it remains a seductive fantasy. It is, moreover, seldom a fantasy that is collectively challenged in mainstream fiction: that task has been taken up by detective fiction.

Notes

1. Peter Worsley, *The Third World* (London, Weidenfeld, and Nicolson, 1969).
2. Kjell Eriksson, *The Demon of Dakar* (London, Allison, and Busby, 2011), p. 366.

3. Herbert Marcuse, 'A Critique of Pure Tolerance' in (eds.) R.P. Wolff, Barrington Moore, Jr., Herbert Marcuse, *A Critique of Pure Tolerance* (Boston, MA, Beacon Press, 1965).

4. Walter Benjamin, 'Theses on the Philosophy of History', *Illuminations* (London, Cape, 1970), pp. 255–67.

5. Michael Lewis, *The Big Short* (London, Penguin, 2010).

6. Jill Leovy, *Ghettoside: Investigating a Homicide Epidemic* (New York, Spiegel, and Grau, 2015).

7. A particularly vivid account of aspects of the making of the 'right to buy' policy is given in Charles Taylor, *Margaret Thatcher: The Authorised Biography*, Vol. 1 (London, Allen Lane, 2013), pp. 262–63, 469–70.

8. For a summary of the global evidence of violence in the home against women see Claudia García-Moreno and Christina Pallitto, *Global and Regional Estimates of Violence against Women: Prevalence and Health Effects of Intimate Partner and Non-Partner Violence* (Geneva, World Health Organisation, 2013).

9. Loretta Lees, *The Emancipatory City: Paradoxes and Possibilities* (London, Sage, 2001).

10. Betty Friedan, *The Feminine Mystique* (New York, W.W. Norton, 1963).

11. Tana French, *Broken Harbour* (London, Hodder, and Stoughton, 2012).

12. Georg Simmel, 'The Mobilisation of Values', *The Philosophy of Money* (London, Routledge, 1978), pp. 505–8.

13. Frank Furedi, *The Culture of Fear* (London and New York, Continuum, 2002).

14. Keith Miller, Review of *Capital* by John Lanchester, *The Daily Telegraph*, 23 February 2012.

15. Rebus accidentally kills the luckless cat Lucky in *Let it Bleed*.

16. William Shaw, *A Song from Dead Lips*, p. 72.

17. *A Song from Dead Lips*, p. 159.

18. *A Song from Dead Lips*, p. 124.

19. *A Song from Dead Lips*, p. 233.

20. *A Song from Dead Lips*, p. 316.

21. *A Song from Dead Lips*, p. 252.

22. *A Song from Dead Lips*, p. 345.

23. Pierre Lemaitre, the author of the *Brigade Criminelle* Trilogy featuring the detective Camille Verhœven.

24. *A Song from Dead Lips*, p. 307.

25. Matthew Frank, *If I Should Die* (London, Penguin, 2014), p. 291.
26. Jean Baudrillard, *The Gulf War Did Not Take Place* (Bloomington, Indiana University Press, 1995).
27. David Mark, the author of the Hull noir series, featuring Detective Sergeant Aector McAvoy.
28. Erik Axl Sund, *The Crow Girl* (London, Penguin, 2016).
29. See, for example, Lisa Cutts, *Remember, Remember* (London, Simon and Schuster, 2014) and Eva Dolan, *Long Way Home* (London, Harvill Secker, 2014).
30. Barbara Ehrenreich, *Fear of Falling: The Inner Life of the Middle Class* (New York, Knopf, 1989).

5

How Do We Connect?

The preceding chapters have sought to demonstrate that post-1970s detective fiction provides important insights into the most pressing collective problems of contemporary social life. This body of literature has provided the basis for discussing, amongst other things, the drive to acquire and demonstrate vast wealth, the weakening hold of traditional ideas about blame and responsibility, the erosion of trust in social authorities and their ability to protect, and the emergence of unpoliceable territories (both virtual and physical). We have suggested that what makes post-1970s detective fiction important as a sociological resource is that it provides an especially vivid, composite picture of these strains, their sources and impacts.

In this chapter we want to suggest something further about the distinctive value of this work. We argue here that this body of literature offers up novel insights about the form of enquiry best suited to identifying and explicating social harm. In other words, these novels provide clues as to how we might connect with the problems of contemporary social life. This is an epistemological matter, as much as anything else. If so much knowledge is withheld or fabricated in post-1970s detective fiction—specifically, official accounts of events and people—this body

© The Author(s) 2019
M. Evans et al., *Detecting the Social*, https://doi.org/10.1007/978-3-319-94520-0_5

of literature offers up alternative bases for knowing what's really going on.

This chapter is partly directed towards unpacking those bases for knowing, and to this end considers how the attributes of literary detectives equip them with the critical faculties needed to engage with the problems of contemporary social life. As much as post-1970s detective fiction asks us to wonder at the abilities of its literary detectives, it at the same time insists upon the risks of accepting singular, exclusive forms of knowledge. As such, a very noticeable feature of many contemporary novels in the genre is that they give voice to a range of characters through a shifting narrative point of view. This represents a significant stylistic shift. Think, for one moment, about the degree to which noir of the mid-twentieth century—the novels of Chandler, Hammett, and others—relies upon the point of view of the detective-protagonist, a perspective that is, to be sure, almost always clouded. Still, the important point here is that these stories are inseparable from the very distinctive voices of Philip Marlowe and Sam Spade. Now think about later, post-1970s detective fiction, and its experiments in de-centring the novel's point-of-view: we have novels that move between the perspective of the police and the victim (to which we return later in this chapter), take us inside the minds of criminals (notably, Karin Fossum's work), and even switch between the various interior worlds of those with split personalities.[1]

The implication of all this is that singular perspectives—even those of a reliable detective-protagonist—aren't revealing in-and-of themselves, and this tells us much about how post-1970s detective novels expect us to connect with the problems it lays before us. In many cases, it means that there is no empirically verifiable solution 'out there', waiting to be discovered by an enquiring mind, but rather complex explanations that can only be partially brought out into the open. Post-1970s detective fiction is keener on disentangling situations and events, than offering exposition. At the same time, this body of literature resists collapsing into relativism and scepticism. It's not, in other words, that there is no 'reality' or 'truth' in post-1970s detective novels—after all, it's a world that is full of very real threats and sources of discomfort—but that the truth is often better-served by deserting any presentiments we might have about who knows best. The shifting narrative point of view serves another function, too, and that is to provide a moral anchor in a world where there is so much confusion about who's to blame—our substantive point of discussion in Chapter 3. Here, we're thinking about the tendency for post-1970s detective fiction to give us access to the point of view of the murderer, and, in this, usually a position and set of sentiments that is clearly abhorrent and worthy of censure. It's one of few certain judgements we can make about who or what is wrong.

We want to add a more general point here: the use of a shifting narrative point of view sheds light on the various ways in which people inhabit the same social world. Post-1970s detective fiction directs particular attention towards the everyday practices by which people accommodate themselves to, and on occasion break free of, structures of power. So it is that these novels are populated by nervy housewives, obsessive compulsives, addicts, the apathetic, hoarders, the overly-orderly—as well as runaways, non-conformists, and vigilantes.

In sketching out these varied ways of making, making-do-with, and resisting the social order, the contemporary detective novel asks us to think about the intimate connection between the individual and society. Indeed, this is the core theme of a notable number of contemporary detective fiction series. Take, for example, Henning Mankell's interest in capturing the impacts of rapid social change on communities. His Wallander series can be read as an extended consideration of the effect of large-scale, rapid social shifts on everyday life, most importantly the accelerated growth of an immigrant population.[2]

In Mankell's novels, and elsewhere, this connection between the individual and society warrants urgent attention, for what's at stake is personal safety—always here a deep, visceral, nerve-jangling concern. That much post-1970s detective fiction sets out to instil fear is only part of the effect here: this body of literature tends also to raise critical questions about what constitutes safety in the first place, something we attend to below. For now, we want to simply point out that the concerns of post-1970s noir, as briefly sketched out above, extend far beyond crime, as it's conventionally understood, at least. If Golden Age detective fiction customarily starts with a problem and ends with a solution—this, at least, is how W. H. Auden (1948) characterises its story arc[3]: post-1970s detective novels typically start with a specific problem, which presages an even bigger and indissoluble problem that is social in character, and, as such, rarely criminal in the legal sense of the word. Chapter 3 was concerned with this idea and linked it to the diffusion of responsibility and blame in post-1970s detective fiction. We'll add, here, that this body of fiction's interest in 'social' guilt means it is at odds with—even, signals its critique of—the idea, so central to late modernity, that the buck stops with the individual. It's an idea that is especially central to the orthodoxy of neo-liberalism, where both prosperity and adversity are, essentially, a matter of individual responsibility.

In asking us to see beyond lines of individual action, post-1970s noir differs markedly from previous forms of detective fiction. Take, by way of contrast, the standard concerns of Golden Age fiction. Where Christie gives us stories of murder and theft, post-1970s detective fiction directs our attention towards the mechanisms for wealth-creation and the social institutions that promote violence. Where Golden Age fiction suggests that the origin of crime lies in the individual (albeit in drives that are common to us all, such as greed, pride, and envy), post-1970s novels ask us to see crime as endemic and caused, in the broadest sense of the word, by a range of social forces and factors. In doing so, they take us beyond, below, deeper, to another level of analysis: and these metaphors are there in the novels themselves. Much of the action in post-1970s detective fiction takes place in subterranean, hidden, or virtual spaces, such as secret rooms and cellars, abandoned high-rises, underground networks of tunnels, and, of course, the internet.

If post-1970s detective novels invite us to think about the possibility that the world in full sight is controlled by, or a product of unseen forces, they suggest that the only way of detecting what's really going on is to be able to see cracks and gaps, omissions and anomalies. To understand the detective novel as Siegfried Kracauer does, as being about concrete, discrete events and effects, and thereby narrow in its moral concerns and vision, is to miss this point.[4] The literary detective must establish a tapestry of *plausible* and *possible* events against which the main act and event is assessed. Thus, we often find in detective fiction an articulation of what is conventional and expected. In contemporary detective fiction, this is often linked to the literary detective's everyday patterns of consumption—eating, drinking, buying newspapers and clothes (that never quite do the job). As discussed in Chapter 4, much of this works to signal the literary detective's failure or refusal to conform to habits of healthy living. It also demonstrates that they are attuned to a world organised around routine. And, of course, that the routines of consumption are so integral to everyday life—can come to stand, even, for everyday life—is in itself important.

To return to our more general point here: the literary detective's job involves a deep knowledge of the mundane. The central criminal event is either a disruption of normal social life (causing, as is famously the case in *Hounds of the Baskerville*, a usually noisy dog to remain quiet) or, more troublingly, a product of it—and this is the mode of critical enquiry most often found in post-1970s detective fiction. Both possibilities require the literary detective to have a firm understanding of everyday life and the forces, both immediate and distant, that maintain its normal functioning. They're people like Thomas Rydahl's ageing, reclusive taxi driver-come-detective, Erhard, 'who've done the same things, over and over…without deviation' (Rydahl 2016: 4), listening, watching, accumulating a stock of knowledge about the routine and the ordinary. Or they're people like Yrsa Sigurðardóttir's workaholic lawyer-detective Þóra Guðmundsdóttir, who can spot and decode an irregular entry in an official record by virtue of having seen so many that fit the norm.

To put it differently, the literary detective is someone who is adept at noticing matter out of place, to borrow from Mary Douglas.[5] This means having a firm understanding of what it means for things to be 'in place', and the forces—normative and pathological, sometimes both at once—that make people stray from convention or routine. In post-1970s detective fiction, this ability to read the social world does not rely upon any formal training or prior experience in detection. Indeed, one thing that marks contemporary novels out is their use of amateur detectives, people thrown into detection by chance, for the sake of self-preservation, to assist a loved one, or out of a sense of empathy. Take, for example, Karin Alvtegen's detective-protagonist Sybilla Forsenstrom, a homeless woman driven to solve a set of murders to clear her name. Or there's Amer Anwar's ex-con-turned-detective Zaq Khan in *Western*

Fringes (2017), forced by his boss to trawl the backstreets of west London to search out his missing daughter.

Despite being green to the task of criminal detection, the amateur detective of post-1970s novels tends to possess qualities that make him or her well-suited to the job in hand. They are especially likely to be lawyers (Åsa Larsson's Rebecka Martinsson, Yrsa Sigurðardóttir's Þóra Guðmundsdóttir), journalists (Thomas Enger's Henning Juul, Stieg Larsson's Mikael Blomkvist, Colin Bateman's Dan Starkey), and hackers (Stieg Larsson's Lisbeth Salander, Christopher Brookmyre's Sam Morpeth). This tells us something about the nature of the problems encountered in post-1970s detective fiction, and the types of skills required to work out what happened. First, amateur detectives' working-lives equip them with a set of advanced investigative skills for interpreting swathes of information. Transposed into the realm of detection, these skills allow for the accessing and the decoding of the two most important sources of evidence in contemporary detective fiction: records of global flows of money and financial connections, and confidential, state-owned databases.

Secondly, amateur detectives' professional roles predispose them to seeing the truth as manufactured—lawyers, journalists, and hackers are, after all, centrally concerned with uncovering back-stories and challenging official accounts. In turn, today's amateur detectives tend to have a professional interest in finding out what happened that is detached from the demands and interests of the state. Indeed, much of the action in these novels stems from the detective's struggle to unravel and counteract the version of events that has been accepted by the police, and other state agencies. As an aside here, it's worth noting that this endeavour can only appear valuable—plausible, even—in a culture where information from formal sources is regularly seen as tainted; as at best spin, at worst fake news. Thus, the amateur detective's ability to see past and challenge the official line is central to their authority to detect the problems of twenty-first century life. Or, put differently, such characters don't suffer from the same problem of institutional distrust that surrounds the contemporary literary police detective. Indeed, if amateur detectives have come to play a more central role in post-1970s detective fiction, we can note here another, related pattern, and that is the recurring problem of public distrust for their professional peers working in the police force. Here, the problem of trust encompasses not just a lack of faith in the factual basis for police investigations, but also a deeply entrenched suspicion that police officers are far from being disinterested keepers of the peace. John Harvey's Charlie Resnick series—set in Nottingham, middle England—is an especially vivid depiction of this type of distrust.[6] Here, members of the local community routinely squirm and protest when the police show up. And we learn that their distrust is well-placed. Take, for example, *Darkness Darkness* (2014), the last novel in the series. The action is split between the present day and the period of the miner's strike during the mid-1980s, as Resnick returns to an old case, the disappearance of a politically-active miner's wife. It's a case that the police struggled to solve—and partly because the community didn't trust the police enough to discuss events surrounding the disappearance. And we learn that this suspicion was well-founded: Resnick himself was involved in undercover police surveillance of the miners. In thinking back, an older, more mature—more twenty-first century—Resnick can see clearly that the police were part of the problem.

Amateur detectives are, of course, free of this institutional baggage, and this often means they're able to see more clearly and think more critically, in the world of the post-1970s detective novel, at least. The third, and final attribute that makes them especially well-suited to the task of detection is that they tend to belong to professional communities that are discrete, rule-bound, and self-regulating. In a social world where the forces of social regulation can seem less persistent and troublesome than in previous historical periods, literary detectives' obedience to (or, at least, consciousness of) professional norms, rules, and expectations is striking. They inhabit communities where the ties that bind the individual to the group are palpable, and the costs of erring are demonstrable. Even the most seemingly individualistic amateur detective—Stieg Larsson's hacker-detective Lisbeth Salander, for example—is keenly aware that social belonging means obeying certain rules, the most effective policing is carried out by a community itself, and group membership is hard-won. This deep social knowledge is part of the skill-set of the contemporary literary detective and shared also by many of the police detectives that feature in this body of literature. They, too, after all, belong to professional communities that are tightly bound by rules, as well as formal and informal forms of regulation. In fact, in novels that focus on police-work, a community of detectives or investigators is often vividly sketched: here we have a social world in miniature, with relationships shaped by disenchantment, secrecy, loyalty, prejudice, status, and ambition. The implication is that police detectives are subject to the same set of social pressures and structures that provide the basis for violence, neglect, and avarice in the world beyond the police station.

There's a broader point to make here: post-1970s detective fiction offers up a set of explorations into how social groups work and flounder. A significant number of novels are specifically interested in close-knit communities, and the types of informal justice and policing that underwrites the social order therein. We're thinking, for example, of Karin Fossum's novels set in remote Norwegian villages and Ann Cleeves' Jimmy Perez stories, based in the Shetland Isles. Of course, Golden Age detective fiction too has a keen interest in small communities—Miss Marple's village of St. Mary Mead, for instance—but the social milieu is implicated quite differently in crime. There is a persistent, if implicit, joke in many of Christie's Miss Marple stories that nothing remains a secret for very long in St. Mary Mead. Things come to light because the regular members of close-knit communities notice and relay things. By contrast, small communities in today's detective novels are more likely to be complicit in hiding the telling details of a crime because bringing things to light compromises, rather than safeguards, the status quo.

In this sense, restoring order is something about which most post-1970s literary detectives are deeply ambivalent, recognising as they do that the structures that underpin social life can be part of the problem. This set of concerns is particularly well illustrated in the treatment of missing people in contemporary detective fiction. The missing person is one of the most notable features of post-1970s detective fiction, as important to the genre today as the locked room mystery was to earlier detective novels. A missing person starts the action in Stieg Larsson's Millennium series, three of Mankell's Wallander novels, Jussi Adler-Olsen's *Mercy*, Michel Bussi's most recent detective novel, *Don't Let Go*,

Sara Blædel's 'missing persons trilogy', and all of Tim Weaver's David Raker novels, focussing as they do on the work of a missing persons investigator. Such is the importance of the convention of the missing person, that it has spawned a sub-genre of its own: the 'gone girl' story, popularised by Gillian Flynn in her 2014 novel of the same name, and then taken up again by Paula Hawkins in *The Girl on the Train* (2016).

It's worth pausing here to note the peculiarity of the missing person as a narrative device. If earlier detective fiction classically started with an eruption of violence—made clear in the bloodied corpse on the drawing room carpet, that most horrifying sign of excess—today's detective fiction tends to start with an omission. In other words, we start with an absence, rather than the presence of a problem. Any reader or viewer of contemporary detective fiction will be deeply familiar with the iconography of absence that signals a missing person in post-1970s noir, and other genres of twenty-first century fiction. Signs of struggle, chores abandoned, an unanswered phone, eerie silence. It's a vanishing akin to a magic act, a sudden tear in the fabric of everyday life.

The effect is deep confusion, first about how someone has disappeared without a trace—this, with all the satellite-enabled technology of the twenty-first century, is as mystifying as the locked room mystery in its seeming impossibility. And secondly, bewilderment concerning the nature of the problem: did someone choose to go missing, or were they taken? It's a plot device that chimes, too, with real-world concerns. We're thinking specifically about the social panics concerning missing children that have become such an important feature of news reporting over the past two decades. In both cases, the missing person unsettles our ideas about safety, whether that's the public safety that makes it possible for children to be thought secure around strangers, or safety within the confines of our homes.[7] For in the many cases where there is doubt about why someone has disappeared in a post-1970s detective novel, and the culture more broadly, we're asked to consider the possibility that home-life can be the source of the problem. This requires a particular way of reading events and characters—for us, as much as the literary detective—that means remaining forever alert to the fine-line between love and toxic intimacy. It also means recognising the existence of tensions and inequalities that make the domestic sphere a place where violence is possible in the first place. And it's worth noting here that there is an unmistakeable pattern to those who go missing in post-1970s detective fiction. In this way, and others besides, we learn that the perils of domestic life aren't evenly shared but are encountered mainly by women and children.

Sara Blædel's *The Killing Forest* (2017) makes this point especially effectively.[8] Blædel's Danish detective fiction series focuses on the work of Louise Rick, a detective in a missing persons investigation unit. *The Killing Forest* starts, like much post-1970s detective fiction, with a missing person, in this case a fifteen-year-old boy, Sune Frandsen. It's clear that his disappearance is part of a much bigger problem concerning a close-knit community of ancient Nordic worshippers. His disappearance was prompted by an initiation ceremony, led by his father, in the local forest. As it becomes clear to Sune that his initiation into the world of 'men' must involve raping a woman, he runs—and watches on as his father and friends assault the woman and call on him to do the same. It's a horrifying episode, not least of all because of the suggestion that fathers are responsible for teaching male sexual violence as a rite of passage. In this respect, the domestic sphere is very much implicated in the wrongdoing that goes on in this novel; or, at least, understanding why people do the things they do necessitates understanding how families operate, the roles and hierarchies they set in place, and the loyalty they demand.

The work the family does to sustain a particular type of social order is often key, then, to working out what's going on in a given situation in post-1970s detective fiction. Families do especially important work in *keeping people in their place*. What we learn, time and again, in contemporary detective fiction, is that this social integration is underwritten by implied and actual violence. Take, by way of example, Åsa Larsson's first book, *The Savage Altar*. The novel centres on Rebecka Martinsson, a high-flying lawyer, returning to her home town to support and represent an old friend who has been accused of killing her brother, a charismatic church leader. At every turn in this novel, we find women being controlled by men, whether that's the accused woman's reliance on the church elders, the killer's long-suffering mother, or even Rebecka Martinsson herself. We learn that she left town as a young woman after having been sexually assaulted by a church elder.

In a key episode in the novel, the local police detective, Anna-Marie Mella, visits the accused's parents. There are no material clues discovered; what she finds instead—and is no less pivotal to understanding what's going on—is a household tightly controlled by a father. Mella spots it immediately in the curious habits of the wife, whose nervy conscientiousness betrays a fear that any minor infraction of the household rules will elicit a telling-off. What's being detected here is how people accommodate themselves (willingly or otherwise) to a particular social order, and what these acts of accommodation tell us about the nature and bases of that order. Post-1970s detective fiction is alive to the possibility for change and subversion in all of this, too. This is another narrative function of the missing person, for we frequently find that those who go missing have absented themselves from a situation at precisely the point at which their willingness to put up with things has worn thin and their instinct for self-preservation has won-out. In *The Savage Altar*, Rebecka Martinsson flees the local community at precisely such a moment. It's not without loss. She's set adrift from a community that, just months before, seemed utterly benevolent. This revelation—that a sense of belonging can be the basis for manipulation, control and violence—is a characteristic feature of post-1970s detective fiction.

Detecting these possibilities—as Mella and Martinsson both do in *The Savage Altar*—means having the ability to see the world in a certain way. There are two main predisposing characteristics that provide literary detectives of post-1970s novels with this critical faculty. The first is experience of domestic life. Attentive readers may well point out here that today's literary detectives tend to be an abject failure when it comes to managing intimate relationships. Nonetheless, we stray into these detectives' home-worlds much more frequently than was the case in earlier detective fiction, and their domestic lives have much more of a bearing on the action of the novels. We're thinking here of, amongst others, Kurt Wallander, whose relationships to both father and daughter loom large in most of Mankell's novels, of Mikael Blomkvist, whose intimate relationships tell us so much about his liberal values, and Hanne Wilhelmsen, the detective-protagonist of Anne Holt's Norwegian crime series, whose desire to keep her sexuality secret is a key source of tension.

Mella is this type of detective too—that is, one who is entangled in domestic life, her intuition as a detective all the more well-honed for it. She's a mother of two and heavily pregnant in *The Savage Altar*, and we're made acutely aware of her responsibility for running a household. We're asked to see these aspects of her life as fundamentally important to her skills as a detective. For one thing, she's able to see that the domestic sphere can breed deep unhappiness and resentment, and what happens here is not incidental to acts of violence elsewhere. For another, she understands that a sense of duty in one sphere of life can have perverse consequences in another. This is a persistent, nagging concern for Mella: she worries that being a good cop might mean being a terrible mother. This is closely related to another problem—and it's shared by so many female literary detectives of the post-1970s period—and that is a desire, always thwarted, to be her own woman.[9] In this case, it manifests itself as a wish to be a mother first, and, at alternating points, a police detective first. The result, of course, is a feeling of being neither first, and therefore nothing absolutely. Here, and elsewhere, the perceived loss is a sense of personal autonomy.

In fact, we know that Mella is a better detective for all of this. For one thing, moving between different social roles means she is able to see the contingency and personal costs of social order. It means she's able to recognise that people are rarely one thing, and one thing only—for example, and in this case, that a much-celebrated pastor can be an abusive brother and uncle. Not, as might have been the case in earlier forms of detective fiction, because people are adept at pretending to be something they're not, but because the values of public life are so frequently at odds with the care and commitment required in our intimate lives. The most publicly successful individuals in post-1970s detective fiction are almost inevitably exceptionally cruel parents and siblings.

Of course, not all detectives in post-1970s novels are attentive to the problems that stem from intimate relationships and family roles. In other cases, what invests a detective with the ability to see what's going on is their experience of loss and victimisation. This, too, is something that distinguishes contemporary detective fiction. If previous detective fiction has emphasised similarities between the detective and criminal—hard boiled fiction of the mid-twentieth century, especially so—contemporary noir is more likely to suggest a connection between the detective and victim.

Stieg Larsson's protagonist, Lisbeth Salander, is the quintessential example here, but she's by no means an isolated case. Abused and neglected as a child, detained by the state on false pretences, and raped by her legal guardian, Salander is deeply suspicious of those with power, especially men. It's a predisposition that gives her the necessary gut instinct for tracking down those inclined towards extreme acts of violence. So, too, with other literary detectives of the post-1970s era. We're thinking here of, amongst others, Sarah Hilary's detective-protagonist, Detective Inspector Marnie Rome, whose parents are brutally murdered, Lisa Cutts' Detective Constable Nina Foster, who was kidnapped as a child, and Pierre Lemaitre's detective-protagonist Commander Camille Verhœven, whose pregnant wife's kidnapping and murder is the subject of the first novel in the Verhœven series.

And beyond these striking cases of victimisation, we find a very significant number of literary detectives who have suffered injustices of one sort or another. They might have been overlooked for promotion by virtue of belonging to a particular social group, as in the case of Adrian McKinty's Catholic detective-protagonist Sean Duffy. Or they've been ostracised from a community, as is the case with Åsa Larsson's Rebecka Martinsson. Or they've been unfairly sanctioned for telling the truth, and here examples abound—Stieg Larsson's Mikael Blomkvist, Alain Massie's Superintendent Lannes, and Jo Nesbø's Harry Hole, to name a few.

None of these literary detectives identify as a victim—indeed, resistance to the idea of being a victim is key to their characterisation—and they often struggle to empathise with the victims with whom they come into contact.[10] What their experiences of victimisation endow them with is a keen understanding of what it means to be subject to the worst excesses of power, and the range of feelings that accompany this: exhaustive anger, deep fear, vengeance, contempt, as well as—for some—forgiveness. In this, and so many other ways, post-1970s detective fiction is a contemplation of what powerlessness does to people. We return to this in due course. For now, we want to make a more general observation: post-1970s detective fiction's enquiries into victimisation contribute to its deeply visceral quality. These are stories of danger and jagged feelings, where simply being in the world is a physical burden. Characters routinely get cold to the bone, live in squalor, get rained-on, go hungry, are beaten up, tortured, self-harm, over-indulge, suffer the niggling pain of clothes worn for the benefit of someone else, and feel the stiffness of old injuries. It's a world of discomfort and, at times, physical duress and pain; a hard, material reality.

Nowhere is the difficulty of being in the world made clearer than in post-1970s detective fiction's exploration of safety. Lisa Cutts' series of UK-based novels featuring Inspector Nina Foster is a case in point. We learn that Foster's experience of having been kidnapped as a child formatively shapes her approach to police-work. Adept at sensing danger—registered by hair standing on end, sudden upsurges of pure fear, and a sensory perception that is almost animalistic—Foster's world is structured around an elemental desire for safety. Her original protector, the police officer who rescued her all those years ago, is an important figure in all of this, as are her daily rituals of checking her home and car. Cutts' novels are centrally concerned with the routines and procedures of police-work: transposed into Foster's personal habits, they become directed towards constant vigilance. The gain is safety, but the cost is deep tiredness, isolation, and fear.

All of this seems at odds with a long-cherished idea in sociology that late modernity has ushered in an era where materialist concerns no longer predominate. The argument runs like this: in the first half of the twentieth century, Europeans' main concerns were of a material nature, namely poverty and need. Greater stability and prosperity in the post-Second World War period meant that ideational, or post-material, concerns came to predominate in the second half of the twentieth century, signalled by the emergence of movements around environmentalism, human rights, and equality.[11]

If post-1970s detective fiction points towards the renewed importance of materialist concerns, it also suggests that these concerns are based on a conception of the relationship between the individual and society that makes it distinct from twentieth century materialism. The sources of concern in the old materialism—poverty and need—were inextricably linked to the state's willingness and ability to protect.

In the new materialism of the twenty-first century, the key source of concern—safety—appears to be most effectively dealt with through vigilance and, on occasion, vigilantism. The answers, in other words, lie in individual action. The world conjured up in post-1970s detective fiction is often a distinctly lonely place, where individuals must face-down danger on their own.

We return to this theme in due course. For now, we want to note that what makes the problem of personal safety especially acute is that the threats it answers to appear difficult to locate. Cutts' portrayal of Nina Foster is again illuminating here, because she perceives herself to be generally, on an almost constant basis, at risk of violence. And the discovery that she has been unknowingly stalked and photographed for many years seems to confirm the suspicion—ours, as well as hers—that this ever-alertness to danger is necessary. Elsewhere, in post-1970s detective fiction, threats to personal safety are not just diffuse, but also deeply unpredictable. The persistent suggestion is that violence could erupt at any point, from anywhere, and without warning or explanation. Take, for example, Henning Mankell's eighth novel, *Firewall* (2003—originally 1998), which conjures up a world where invisible currents of mischief—here, it's an online group of cybercriminals bent on enforcing changes to global capitalism—create random spasms of violence. The novel starts with a set of seemingly unrelated murders, all of them inexplicable acts of violence. They're followed by large-scale power cuts and computer malfunctions, stemming from a radical anti-capitalist group's attempt to bring about a total breakdown of the existing social order. The result is a general pull of everything towards oblivion, an anarchism that is so unpredictable and ambitious that the police can offer little in the way of protection. "We live in a vulnerable society", the police forensics expert Nyberg muses in assessing the ensuing chaos (Mankell 2003: 82).[12] It's a sentiment that chimes with the pervading sense of insecurity we find in post-1970s noir.

In some ways, post-1970s detective fiction takes aim at this—confirming that, after all, the most likely sources of danger are close at hand—and in other senses it shines a light on the peculiar brand of fear that pertains in late modern societies. A central feature of this is a sense that nowhere and no one is safe, and that even the most intimate parts of one's personal life can be infiltrated. As such, there is a persistent suggestion in contemporary detective novels that danger can creep into the seemingly safe recesses of our homes and personal lives. The narrative device of the missing person contributes to this overall effect, as it frequently involves victims being plucked from their homes. So, too, does the recurring motif of the telephone ringing in the middle of the night, usually interrupting the detective's peaceful sleep or dream, and bringing terrible news. It's a convention that indicates the detective's constant accessibility as well as the possibility for a world of danger and chaos to reach into (and wake them up from) a place of safety. Consider too the regularity with which detectives' homes become crime scenes—perhaps most evocatively conjured up in Sarah Hilary's *Someone Else's Skin*, where the detective arrives on the scene to find her childhood home cordoned off by police ticker tape, her parents the victims of a double homicide.[13]

There are other ways in which we might see post-1970s detective fiction as a probing consideration of the effects of and conditions for fear in late modern societies. Take, for example, the tendency—so rare in detective novels pre-1970—to give us access to the interior thoughts and feelings of victims. Pierre Lemaitre's French detective novel *Alex* (2013), Jussi Adler-Olsen's Copenhagen-based novel, *Mercy* (2013), and Mick Herron's London-based *Slow Horses* (2015) go particularly far in this. In each of these novels the action is split so that we move between following the police investigation and the victim's experience—a horrific, terrifying ordeal—of being held captive, expecting death at any moment. It's a narrative structure that is meant to invite voyeurism. In Lemaitre's (2013) *Alex*, we are given access to the terrifying experience of a young woman, the eponymous Alex, who has been kidnapped and installed in a cage.[14] Her captor is impervious to her entreaties. All Alex—and we—get from him is a darkly repeated phrase: "I want to watch you die". The gratuitousness and extended nature of the violence indicates that Lemaitre wants us to consider whether we, like Alex's captor, find enjoyment in the spectacle. At the least, there's a connection drawn between the scopic fantasies of reader and captor. Lemaitre pushes this further: when Alex eventually breaks free and unleashes all her raw anger and terror on her captor, it's an act of vengeance that feels at once cathartic and reasonable. After all, we've been stuck in that cage with Alex too.

The achievement of *Alex* is that it asks us to think again about the basis for all this violence in such a way as to challenge any identification we might have had with Alex. It's so easy, in reading this novel, to see this young woman's torture as our own, a nightmarish reminder that there are chaotic, sadistic forces of cruelty in the world. Here we get to nub of it, for *Alex* conjures up—and then challenges—a fear that races through our collective consciousness like a phantom: it's the fear of complete obliteration, slowly-wrought, delivered without meaning and purpose, visited upon those who deserve it least. And, again, the crucial ingredient in all of this is the indiscriminate exercise of power for its own sake. *Alex*, after all, is an extended contemplation of what it means to be subject to someone else's will. In this novel, and so much other detective fiction today, dehumanisation is the chief effect of sadism; here, with Alex kept as a caged animal, that message is explicit.

It's tempting to see the concerns of novels like *Alex* as far-removed from those of the more socially-conscious detective novels of the post-1970s era. *Alex* seems like an intimate portrait of fear and cruelty, meant to erode our sense of safety. The other set of novels seem so resolutely directed towards pushing our attention outwards, to the social relations that give rise to violence. What both types of novel share, though, is a deep concern with the subjugating effect of power, especially when it is wrought indiscriminately and anonymously. If this is the basis for a distinctive pathology in post-1970s detective fiction, we're frequently asked to see particular forms of social organisation as pathogenic, notably patriarchy and late capitalism. And these systems of power frequently coalesce to produce dehumanising violence. Nowhere is this clearer than in contemporary detective fiction's concern with human trafficking for the purposes of sexual exploitation, the focus in Mankell's *Side-tracked*, Larsson's *Millennium Trilogy*, and a number of novels in Sara Blædel's Louise Rick series, to name a few. The transformation of humans into tradable goods is taken here as the apotheosis of capitalism, as is the constant circulation of these 'goods', both geographically and financially. Indeed, it is a striking feature of post-1970s noir that there are very few owners, per se; assets, human or otherwise, simply don't stay immobile long enough. Instead, we have a world of brokers, dealers, and traders. The effect is a radical de-centring of power, or, rather, its diffusion, so that accumulation becomes a boundless project, its beneficiaries and victims obscure.

These are the core themes of Danish writer Peter Høeg's award-winning novel *Miss Smilla's Feeling for Snow* (1993, original 1992), and the novel engages with these ideas in such a way as to enquire into the human costs of capitalist accumulation.[15] Here, the socially-awkward Smilla Jaspersen feels compelled to investigate the suspicious death of her neighbour, six-year-old Isaac, who, according to the police, fell accidentally from a snowy rooftop. The patterns in the snow tell Smilla differently, hence the novel's title. She was born in Greenland, taught Inuit by her mother, and retains a sharp sense of the differences between snow formations. Doggedly pursuing the case, Smilla discovers that Isaac was collateral damage in a Danish corporation's bid to recover a precious meteorite from one of Greenland's islands.

What is shocking about Høeg's novel is not so much that people get killed, but that killing someone can be such a meaningless act. *Alex* raises the same possibility. Indeed, it is a general lesson of post-1970s detective fiction that people can be killed for no good reason, or, worse still, no reason at all. All this makes the ending of *Miss Smilla's Feeling for Snow* interestingly ambiguous. We're left with Smilla chasing an assailant out to sea, into likely mutual obliteration. There's no closure to be found here, no demonstrative payback for the heinous crime of thoughtlessly murdering a child. Instead, we're left considering other, less direct types of remedy—for one, that the act of pursuing is its own reward. Perhaps, in a world so devoid of meaning, there is less valour in apprehending a murderer than in doggedly pursuing the truth. The former answers to a specific problem, the latter to a more general feature of the human condition, that is, the fear of meaninglessness.

There are other countervailing forces in Høeg's novel, most notably, Smilla's native language and traditions. Her Inuit heritage is something Smilla's Danish father sees as devoid of utility. It certainly appears to have no use at all in the context of late capitalist, post-industrial Denmark; but it can, we find, invest the world with nuances of meaning that are otherwise lacking. Utility and meaning exist in an inverse relationship throughout this novel, with the former inextricably linked to capitalism and deeply corrosive in its effects. So, towards the end of the novel, Smilla decides that the root of the problem is the existence of an urge 'stronger than any empathy for living things: the desire for money' (Høeg 1993, 404). Her point—and that of the novel more generally—is that the profit motive involves a single-mindedness; nothing other than a calculable growth in capital registers or matters, least of all human life. That the action in Høeg's novel moves from a local neighbourhood (in this case, in Copenhagen) to the wide expanses of the Arctic Ocean gets at something really important about this core dynamic of capitalism. As we travel further into the uninhabitable regions of our world, further away from human life, the explanation for Isaac's death becomes clearer: it lies in the unstoppable, unceasing force of capitalist expansion, horribly rational in its determination to push on at any cost, and terrifyingly wild in its unassailability and destructiveness. It's a force beyond nature, even. This suggests another, less hopeful reading of the ending of Høeg's novel. After all, the ending recalls that of Mary Shelley's *Frankenstein*, that great, portentous late nineteenth century novel. Here, too, we end with a desperate chase through icy hinterlands—this time Frankenstein chasing the monster that has got so far beyond his control. The association is suggestive, because in both novels the grand chase is the product of impossible dreams of living beyond our natural limits.[16] Both novels raise the question 'What have we created?'

The other thing to say about the ending of *Miss Smilla's Feeling for Snow* is that it focuses our attention on Smilla's aloneness and precariousness. Indeed, what's striking about the world conjured up in post-1970s detective fiction is the degree to which individuals are expected to face-down problems alone. We touched upon this above, in discussing the way in which post-1970s detective fiction alights upon the problem of personal safety as the predominant materialist concern of the twenty-first century. It's there too in the emphasis on vigilantism and vigilance, distinctly individualised responses to danger and violence. And it's evident also in the almost complete absence of protection for those individuals who strike out to resolve matters. We're thinking of protection broadly here, to include not just the work done by criminal justice agencies, but sources of social protection. The latter is an important theme in post-1970s detective fiction. Here, we tend to find a social world that is characterised by the breakdown of the post-war welfare settlement—the pact, on the part of European states, to provide from cradle to grave.[17] It's not just that social workers, police officers, and other state officials routinely fail to get what's really going on in these novels; they are defined also by their absence, incompetence, apathy, and lack of compassion. All this means that the old solutions of social intervention are routinely insufficient and harmful—often laughably so. Take, for example, Karin Alvtegen's Stockholm-based novel, *Missing* (2003). Here, a long-term homeless woman, Sibylla, becomes accidentally caught-up in a set of horrific murders, and is pursued relentlessly by the police as the suspect for the crimes. The intense nature of the media and police attention is in stark contrast to the lack of institutional interest and care for her as a homeless person. As a homeless person she's treated as a non-entity, her sheer visibility taken as an affront. As a suspected criminal, Sibylla is suddenly, and for the first time in her life, a person of public interest, and for all the wrong reasons.

In other ways, too, post-1970s detective fiction is interested in the failure of social institutions to protect. The device of the missing person serves an important function here, demonstrating, as it often does, that institutions lack staying power. What we often find is that the police quickly run aground in their investigation of a missing person and move to drop the case. This lack of impetus is only partly down to a frustrating absence of clues. We're often asked to see it as connected to an institutional culture that places targets ahead of a duty of care, and partly—in some instances, at least—the missing person's lack of social value. Take, again, Alvtegen's detective-protagonist, Sybilla, who, we learn, passed quickly from being missing to permanently homeless, partly because she was roundly seen as troublesome and not worth the effort of pursuing. Two of Massie's four Bordeaux-based detective novels, too, feature the disappearance of young women who are deemed by the police to be not worth finding.

In these cases, and in many other novels besides, it's up to the detective-protagonist to take up the task of pursuing the case independently. These are important interventions in post-1970s detective fiction, not least of all because the willingness of the detective-protagonist to pursue a case beyond it being expedient shows up the limited attention span of official institutions. If institutions readily move on and forget—the sheer abundance of cold cases in post-1970s detective novels demonstrates as much—our detective-protagonist refuses to do so. There's an equivalence, here, to the personal experience of loss, and we're frequently reminded of that: the stock characters of post-1970s detective fiction include parents who have never moved on from the death of a child, people who harbour grudges for decades, and those who develop unhealthy obsessions that speak of an inability to let go. It's not just that modern institutions routinely fail to connect with these emotional reactions; in their readiness to move on, they exacerbate a sense of injustice and leave loose ends. A consistent lesson of post-1970s detective fiction is that institutions bury individual histories, and neglect or miss their real meaning. The answer to this institutional forgetting is a monumental effort of memory-recovery. Post-1970s detective novels often involve the literary detective resolving a case by digging through dusty official files to work out what really happened.[18] It's work that signals the detective's ability to stick with it: to slowly and laboriously locate and reassemble the personal story that lies beyond the case file. And, by contrast, the propensity for institutions to bury and conceal information is framed as symptomatic of deeper social problems— as discussed above, an overall, catastrophic failure to protect, or even care. This antipathy towards bureaucratic systems is, in one sense, well-rehearsed, by, amongst others, Kafka. But post-1970s detective fiction suggests a deepening of the problem in terms of the tendency for bureaucratic systems to neglect those who are most in need of help. To put it simply, we learn time and again that certain people are more likely to be forgotten than others, just like some people are deemed not worth finding.[19]

The literary detective's effort to restore and enliven institutional memory, as with Smilla's pursuit through the icy hinterlands of the Arctic Ocean, is an act that refuses to let the world give way to meaninglessness. In post-1970s detective fiction, the acts of pursuing and remembering both become ways of facing-down the obliterative forces of late modernity, most notably bureaucracy and capitalism. The more general question these novels pose is what people do—can do, should do, tend to do—when they are subject to the worst excesses of power, particularly when the precise cause of loss and pain is difficult to locate. This is why cycles of sadistic, dehumanising violence are such a central feature of the genre today, suggesting, as they do, a desire to replay and repay the experience of subordination. It also helps explain the distinctive tone of post-1970s detective fiction, namely its visceral quality, and particularly its emphasis on raw anger, fear, and vengeance. It's an emotional repertoire for our times, most often expressed through a desire to reclaim an expressive, retributive form of justice. Sociologists and cultural commentators have only just begun to consider the social bases and costs of this wave of collective fury, prompted, no doubt, by the rise of populist politics—the most striking, troublesome embodiment of these emotional reactions, for now, at least. Post-1970s detective fiction has been connecting with the problems of contemporary social life for far longer, and in such a way as to suggest that we should look to the operation of power in late modern societies, and the particular condition of powerlessness it produces.

Notes

1. The Norwegian detective fiction writer Karin Fossum has gone especially far in giving access to the literary murderer's narrative point of view. In her 2004 novel, *The Murder of Harriet Krohn*, for example, the story is told from the murderer's perspective.
2. See, in particular, *Faceless Killers* (1997), *The Dogs of Riga* (2001), *Side-tracked* (1999).
3. W.H. Auden's 1948 essay in *Harper's* magazine sets out to explain his love of detective fiction. In doing so, he charts a standard story arc for mid-twentieth century, Golden Age detective fiction (he's thinking, in particular, of Christie's novels), where a false sense of security and harmony is followed by an eruption of violence, then by a false accusation, and then, finally, the uncovering of the perpetrator and a movement to genuine security and harmony.
4. See Frisby's (1992) discussion of Kracauer.
5. Mary Douglas' suggestion, in *Purity and Danger* (2003, originally 1966), is that we understand dirt as 'matter out of place'. The idea isn't unique to her, but she develops it in a novel way, suggesting that

cultural responses to things and people we perceive to be 'dirt' or 'dirty' reflect our deeply-entrenched desire to keep the normal intact. For Douglas, our concerns around dirt speak of a collective fear that the spaces and ideas that we cherish will be polluted.

6. Ethnicity and multiculturalism are also key sources of conflict between the police and local community in John Harvey's Charlie Resnick series (see, for example, *Cold in Hand*, 2008). This distrust works both ways in Harvey's novels: local ethnic minority communities resent the police, and we're repeatedly shown that the police are suspicious of ethnic minority groups. The latter comes out particularly in the treatment of black police officers by their white colleagues. Harvey's interest in police racism—directed inwards or outwards—contributes to an overall impression that professional detective-work is impaired by certain biases.

7. There is a significant sociological literature on the social panic of missing children—see, for example, Critcher (2010), and, for an analysis of US news and culture, Jenkins (1998).

8. The trope of the missing person has been taken up in detective fiction beyond Europe, to become a key feature of post-1970s detective novels worldwide. Take, for example, Sara Paretsky's first novel, *Indemnity Only* (1982). Here we are introduced to V.I. Warshawski, a Chicago-based private detective, and the female protagonist for Paretsky's hugely popular, award-winning series of detective novels. Indemnity Only starts, like much post-1970s noir, with a missing person, Anita. And despite the novel's ostensible focus on the grimy world of management and unionised labour, much of the action is focussed on the relationships and structure of two families, with their social class differences and aspirations finely-drawn. The work of tracing Anita serves to unravel these relationships.

9. This problem of personal autonomy is a persistent one for female detectives in post-1970s detective fiction. It's there, for example, in Yrsa Sigurðardóttir's characterisation of Þóra Guðmundsdóttir, for whom the balance between work and intimate relationships is an ongoing struggle.

10. There's a broader cultural trend here to give space and attention to victims' stories. We're thinking, for example, of the emergence of autobiographical accounts of abuse as a distinct genre in the twenty-first century, as well as the more towards a more victim-centred criminal

justice system (exemplified by the reading of victim impact statements at criminal trials).

11. See Inglehart (1990).

12. There is a sizeable sociological literature on a new, collective feeling of vulnerability, most of which points to its limited relationship to empirical reality—see, for example, Furedi (2003) and Best (1999).

13. A related trend is evident in the re-emergence of the home invasion film in the twenty-first century and its focus on anarchic, motiveless—and therefore deeply horrifying—violence (Jones 2016).

14. *Alex* is the second book in Pierre Lemaitre's Camille Verhœven series. As of 2018, the series consists of three novels, all of which have been nominated for the CWA International Dagger award, and two have won (*Alex*, and the third novel in the series, *Camille*).

15. Peter Høeg's *Miss Smilla's Feeling for Snow* is one of the most successful detective novels of the twenty-first century. It won the Crime Writer's Association Silver Dagger Award and was shortlisted for an Edgar Award.

16. In Shelley's *Frankenstein*, the dream of reaching beyond our natural limits is connected to the unchecked ambition of science. *Miss Smilla's Feeling for Snow* takes aim at science too, but here the drive for scientific discovery is given additional impetus by the desire for corporate expansion.

17. Much has been written about the decline of the post-Second World War welfare settlement—see, for example, Hughes and Lewis (1998). Whilst it's true that there are significant variations between European countries' welfare state arrangements, there has evidently been a general trend of retrenchment.

18. John Harvey's *Frank Elder* series is partly distinguished by the detective-protagonist's commitment to return to and pursue cases that have long been shelved. All three of these novels—a fourth is due out after the publication of this book—focus on Elder, a retired police officer, being pulled back into re-examine old cases that went unsolved.

19. It's a problem that, again, extends into the real-world, where, for example, a group of UK citizens of Caribbean descent—the so-called Windrush generation—have been systematically disenfranchised because of changes to institutional rules and practices to make the UK a more 'hostile environment' for migrants.

References

Alvtegen, Karin. 2003. *Missing*. UK: Felony and Mayhem.

Auden, Wystan Hugh. 1948. The Guilty Vicarage: Notes on the Detective Story, by an Addict. *Harper's*, May, 406–412.

Best, Joel. 1999. *Random Violence: How We Talk about New Crimes and Victims*. Berkeley: University of California Press.

Critcher, Chas. 2010. Media, Government, and Moral Panic: The Politics of Paedophilia in Britain 2000–1. *Journalism Studies* 3 (4): 521–535.

Douglas, Mary. 2003 (originally 1966). *Purity and Danger: An Analysis of Concepts of Pollution and Taboo*. London: Routledge.

Frisby, David. 1992. Between the Spheres: Siegfried Krakauer and the Detective Novel. *Theory Culture, Society* 9 (1): 1–22.

Furedi, Frank. 2003. *Therapy Culture: Cultivating Vulnerability in an Uncertain Age*. London: Routledge.

Harvey, John. 2008. *Cold in Hand*. London: Carroll & Graf Publishers.

Høeg, Peter. 1993. *Miss Smilla's Feeling for Snow*. UK: Farrar, Straus and Giroux Inc. and the Harvill Press.

Hughes, G., and G. Lewis. 1998. *Unsettling Welfare: The Reconstruction of Social Policy*. London: Routledge.

Inglehart, Ronald F. 1990. *Culture Shift in Advanced Industrial Society*. Princeton, NJ: Princeton University Press.

Jenkins, P. 1998. *Moral Panic: Changing Concepts of the Child Molester in Modern America*. New Haven, CT: Yale University Press.

Jones, M. 2016. A Room Going Spare: Lodgers, Nannies, and Strangers in the Home. In *Spaces of the Cinematic Home: Behind the Screen Door*, ed. E. Andrews, S. Hockenhull, and F. Pheasant-Kelly, 167–179. London: Routledge.

Mankell, Henning. 2003. *Firewall*. UK: The Harvill Press.

Paretsky, Sara. 1982. *Indemnity Only*. London: Hodder and Stoughton.

Rydahl, Thomas. 2016. *The Hermit*. UK: Point Blank.

6

Conclusion

This book has sought to establish the value of detective fiction in helping us to read and make sense of the social world, at a time when we seem beset by instability and crisis. That detective fiction provides us with such probing and sophisticated enquiries in turn shows up mainstream sociology's relative lack of purchase on the collective problems of social life. The discipline has long recognised that its value as an empirical project is under threat from the expansion of big data, its particular claims to knowledge seeming increasingly out-dated.[1] We think there's another, more pressing, problem for contemporary sociology, and that is its failure to identify and explain the underground fissures of late modernity.

Worse still, sociologists seem no longer to be held accountable for this task. One of the most urgent questions directly after the economic crisis of 2008 was how economists had failed to see it coming.[2] In contrast, no one bemoaned sociologists' lack of foresight in failing to call Brexit, the ascendency of Trump, or populist movements across Europe. And yet, the signs were there. They're there in detective fiction of the last fifty years, which has been tracing out the fault-lines in our social arrangements, rehearsing our collective fears, and capturing a

© The Author(s) 2019   **149**
M. Evans et al., *Detecting the Social*, https://doi.org/10.1007/978-3-319-94520-0_6

mood of restless disquiet. Here, we find enquiries into what happens when institutional power becomes invisible and unassailable, the profit motive becomes all-encompassing, public bodies fail to intervene and protect, and blame and responsibility become difficult to locate. The personal consequences of living like this are made palpably, horrifyingly real in contemporary detective fiction: they are the degradations of the flesh, unproductive searches for personal safety, and eviscerating encounters with the hard, material reality of everyday life.

In asking us to think like this, post-1970s detective fiction conjures up the intimate connections between the individual and society. This is not to suggest that today's literary detective sees the social world in terms of different levels of effect and order—that is, in terms of social structure and, as a separate matter, everyday life. This is how Boltanski (2014) understands detective fiction. He sees the detective novel of the mid-nineteenth century as articulating a collective fantasy of social order, intimately tied to the rise of the modern state. The rhetoric of law and order, Boltanski argues, conjures up the modern citizen as an individual who acts and thinks in certain ways and the modern state as a natural arbiter. This is the 'reality' that literary detectives bring to bear, and in doing so they mould the real world of action and events, the raw material of life.

Detective novels might tell us something about the power of the modern state in forcing a certain conception of the citizen and their behaviour, but they show us something further and, we want to suggest, just as important about how social order is wrought. They show, for example, how the formal interpretation of the relationship between the citizen and the state is transposed by people and communities. They illuminate how the violence that legitimates the modern state is absorbed into people's everyday lives. They suggest the ways in which people accommodate themselves, sometimes on a daily basis, to social order as it is officially conceived, and the often pragmatic work that goes into softening or maintaining a harsh 'reality'. These acts of transposition, absorption, and accommodation are not steps between the realms of 'reality' and the real—we do not wish to conceive of them as simple rejections of or submission to modern institutional arrangements—rather they are meaningful and impactful in and of themselves in creating social order. This is work that sociological accounts too frequently exclude.

This is not to ignore the fact that social theorists have used various forms of Marxism, psychoanalysis, feminism and empiricism in order to suggest—and to attempt to solve—that most mysterious connection between the individual person and the social world in which they live. Yet one thing that is striking about such attempts is that they rarely seek to conjure up social life and, as a central feature of this, the work individuals do to accommodate themselves to the social order. Part of the problem here is that, despite sociology's interest in subjectivity, the individual is generally lightly-sketched. Instead, social order is conceived of as something that is contractual, systemic, or in terms of interactional scaffolding; as something, in other words, that issues from and returns to a point outside of the individual and her immediate sphere of action. More than that, the accounts of social reality provided by sociologists are often—and disappointingly—*unpeopled*. Goffman and Schutz are notable exceptions to this; but here we find a social world that is stripped of its socio-historical co-ordinates and untouched by socially-entrenched differences in power.[3] The individual is most certainly evident in these sociological accounts, but they are placed in a social world that lacks depth and structure beyond the here-and-now. We find the opposite problem in sociological accounts that cross the dialectical divide between human agency and social structure—as, for example, Bourdieu and Bhaskar do. Here, there is no attempt made to bring the individual and her social world to life, to think about what it is like to live in a certain way, and all that this means: with certain rules, in a given place, with particular people, under specific socio-economic conditions.

This task becomes all the more important in studies attending to the pathologies of everyday life. And it's notable here that those social theories which have done the most to inform studies of the social reality of the late twentieth and early twenty-first century—notably Bauman, Bourdieu, Foucault—share an interest in the psychological, and, more than that, the pathological, human condition.[4] But, again, quite how the individual is realised and the circumstances, both personal and social, which are constitutive of his or her reality are seldom explored. It is only the general, collective experience that is examined. What then comes to mind this fracture between the individual and the social is psychoanalytical theory, a theory which—certainly in its canonical form—is premised on a general view of behaviour. But, as with other forms of social theory, psychoanalysis cannot answer questions about individual differences or indeed the very emergence of that pathology which was the motive of its foundation. As we live within more diverse and often contested forms of that condition what becomes increasingly difficult for social theory to explain is the pathological individual.

So general theories, be they of society, the social, or the individual, routinely turn to literature (and other forms of representation) in order to 'bridge the gap' between the epistemological authority of theory and the confusions, contradictions and chaos of everyday life. Implicit to these endeavours is an assumption of radical difference between 'theory' and the 'imagined' that has had all kinds of implications for discussions both inside and outside the academy. Amongst these are the emergence of hierarchical judgements about different genres of literature, with the assumption that only conventional or 'literary' fiction can illuminate the human condition.[5]

Part of our aim in writing this book has been to call such categories into question by confirming detective fiction's value as a form of critical enquiry into the aberrant territory of the modern and the pathologies produced therein. In arguing along these lines, we are suggesting a radically different conception of the sociological value of literature. Conventional sociological accounts of fiction have generally approached it in terms of the ways in which that literature can illustrate, enlarge or help to articulate a particular social theory.[6] From the earliest accounts of fiction in the canonical tradition of Anglo-American social theory this form of relationship has been remarkably consistent, even given the different politics and degrees of sophistication in those accounts.

This book has sought to implement a new form of relationship between fiction and social theory. Here, detective fiction is not taken as a way of illustrating general theories. Rather, this group of novels allows us to detect so far unidentified, but very important, theoretical ideas about what it means to be an individual in the twenty-first century. They also make powerful suggestions concerning how we ought to understand individual action in the first place. For one thing, contemporary detective fiction insists that the individual is best thought of as existing in a dynamic relationship with the world—and that 'world' is, amongst other things, a hard material reality of obstacles, fissures, and toil. This is one reason why straight lines of cause-and-effect aren't much in evidence in post-1970s detective fiction: characters exist in worlds that offer too much resistance, operate according to their own logic, where things (and people) continually get in the way.

Contemporary detective novels achieve this conception of the individual by vividly-sketching social worlds in such a way as to reveal their *social texture.* Texture is a term is widely used within the Arts to refer to the combination of elements to create perceptual depth.[7] The task of the art critic is to discern the elements of the art-work, their relationship and effect; to move, that is, between the part and the whole, and do service to each. The literary detective works in a similar way, and in doing so shows up the importance of texture as a critical tool for making sense of the social world. Indeed, if they were to approach the social world as a structure or a system—the more usual and prized metaphors of social theory—they would forgo an understanding of why some people are driven to do bad things. The literary detective knows that power and status produce hierarchies, but it is their understanding of what it means to be lonely, the strain of pretence, and the possibility that neglect has a cumulative effect that makes them well-placed to understand the different ways in which people can inhabit the same social world.

This book has sought to demonstrate that post-1970s detective fiction is a form of critical enquiry that is peculiarly well-suited to understanding this world, its perversities and pathologies. It is no accident that the most pressing political problems in late modern societies overlap to a striking degree with the concerns of the contemporary detective novel. Both are beset by an empirical problem concerning the veracity of truth-claims, an epistemological problem concerning the possibility of knowing for sure, and a problem of authority concerning who to trust. In the world of the post-1970s detective novel—and, we want to suggest, beyond—these problems often appear so intractable as to produce a peculiar type of powerlessness. Post-1970s detective fiction is particularly concerned with sketching out the range of responses this prompts. This book has sought to identify some of these reactions; they include characters' efforts to rail against meaninglessness, detective-protagonists' frenzied work to counteract the myopia of social institutions, as well as a more diffuse, crushing feeling of anger concerning long-buried truths. These, we think, are key features of the late modern condition.

One of the distinctive achievements of post-1970s detective fiction is that it brings this condition into critical focus, and in such a way as to suggest its relationship with social conditions. We're urged to think not just about what it means to feel powerless, and how one might—or could, should—react, but also how it is that we've come to live in a social world that insists on an accommodation that is all one-way. The city is often key to this: it is, almost inevitably, a place of sheer discomfort that exacerbates and produces a sense of personal powerlessness. The city institutes a way of life and contributes to the prevailing sense that an essential friction exists between the world and the individual. Characters walk for miles, in ill-fitting shoes. They live in tiny apartments with thin walls. Cramming into public spaces, they are thrown into awkward intimacy with strangers. Or they wind up in the deserted spaces of the city—the abandoned tower block, unpoliceable sink estates, or derelict warehouse—and that way, real trouble lies.

If ghettoization is a persistent problem of urban life in post-1970s detective fiction, so is its counterpart: gentrification. We quickly learn that attempts to escape the degradations of city-life signal different types of problems. In some instances, escaping means hiding—only murderers have penthouse suites with secret rooms—and in other instances it means being dangerously sequestered—peril lurks in gated communities and middle-class housing estates. In both cases, the home is associated with a ruinous desire that remains forever unsatiated—it is either the place where pathological sexual desire can be enacted, or the embodiment of a mythical good life. Chapter 4 dealt with these ideas, but here we'll simply point out that each of the living arrangements discussed here—living in the city proper, and attempts to extricate oneself from it—tend to produce a deep sense of homelessness and dislocation that is at best physically draining, and at worst utterly calamitous for the individuals concerned.

The more general observation is that post-1970s detective fiction suggests that *where* people live is inextricably linked to *how* they live. This body of fiction is interested, too, in the invisible social forces that shape our lives—in Society with a capital 'S'. Late capitalism, patriarchy, and bureaucracy are all implicated here, and in such a way as to emphasize the violence done by each (by accident and design), and their horrifying unassailability. Each constitutes an obliterative force in post-1970s detective fiction, not least of all because of a tendency to dehumanize. And those who front-up to these forms of power by bucking rules, or calling out an injustice, are generally subject to the most degrading types of powerlessness. What makes their situation all the more precarious is their treatment by official organizations as inherently untrustworthy and dangerous, as people who have no right to even the most basic form of social protection. In these cases, the official line on someone— that they're 'just' a runaway, a troublemaker, in need of medical control, to be disbelieved, a serial offender—allows for abuse to go unseen and untreated. Post-1970s detective fiction is populated by characters who are set adrift in this way: rootless wanderers, cast aside, forgotten and neglected. It's an experience characterized by everyday humiliations and accumulating injustices that, in the world of post-1970s detective fiction, leads inexorably to an all-encompassing desire for safety, vengeance, and personal freedom. This is more often than not the antidote to a deep sense of powerlessness, and it's rarely without cost—but more on this in due course.

For now, we want to note that whilst all sorts of people can and do find themselves in this situation in post-1970s detective novels, some people are more prone to marginalization than others, notably young women, ethnic minorities, and members of subcultures. And disenfranchisement, once set in motion, is often tied to authoritarian judgements about sexuality, identity, and lifestyle. It's an exercise of social control that serves as an extraordinarily demeaning curtailment to personal autonomy, for 'who someone is' comes to be first officially defined and then formally condemned. And this, in a social context where we seem to have so much more freedom over how we live and our personal identities. Thus, contemporary detective fiction persistently suggests that the power to direct one's life—to choose how to live, free from persecution—is yet another distinguishing feature of the divide between the 'haves' and the 'have nots'.

It's not just the condition of powerlessness that is shaped by social organization in post-1970s detective fiction (and, of course, in the world beyond). Sources of social harm, too, are socially-structured, and particularly along gender lines. For women in post-1970s detective fiction, the single biggest threat is male violence, frequently sexual in nature. For men in post-1970s detective fiction—those, at least, that find themselves subject to harm—threats issue from elsewhere, namely the forces of capitalist expansion and the drive for political power. This is a world where men tend to be the victims of male battles for social control, and women tend to be the victims of (largely male) sexual fantasies. The plight of the literary detective reveals as much. Male detectives are much more likely than their female peers to be involved in a violent struggle over what type of order will win-out (that of the detective, or the aberrant criminal higher-up). Female detectives, in turn, tend to be imperilled by male stalkers and rapists, and their detective work is generally oriented towards untangling the violence wrought by pathological male desire. In other words, it attends to the problems of the domestic sphere.

Thinking along these lines should prompt us to recognise that the problem of safety is qualitatively different for men and women, and more than that, the work of maintaining social order is gendered. The more general observation to make here is that post-1970s detective fiction alerts us to the various ways in which social order is made, sustained, challenged, and on occasion broken. These are peculiarly modern concerns, reflecting the idea that social order is the product of human intention, rather than divine intervention. In this sense, post-1970s detective fiction not only distils contemporary social problems, but also turns our attention to one of the most elemental and enduring problems of modernity.

The problem of social order can be traced back to the European liberal-humanist revolution of the sixteenth century. Michelangelo's *Moses*—as interpreted by Freud (1914)—is a monument to this new humanist conception of social order. Finished in 1515, the sculpture depicts an inscrutable and restless Moses loosely holding the tablets containing God's commandments. Freud contends that Michelangelo has captured the moment Moses descended Mount Sinai, having received the tablets from God, and found his people worshipping a false idol.

For Freud, the unnerving impression that this forever-fixed Moses might at any moment spring forth is an effect of the artist's attempt to render Moses' inner turmoil on discovering his people disobeying God's law. Through a close analysis of the figure's deportment and gestures Freud concludes that what Michelangelo has captured is not the moment of ire upwelling—coterminous with the biblical account, which has Moses take vengeance on his people by dashing the tablets to the floor in rage—but instead a moment of self-control winning out and temper being subdued. In *Exodus*, a punishing Moses brings God-given law to his people and, dismayed at so much sin, withdraws it. Biblical law comes to the Hebrews because God exercises forgiveness and forces Moses to convey the tablets again. In Michelangelo's re-telling, Moses battles with himself and decides to deliver social order. Biblical law comes to the Hebrews because Moses allows it to. In doing so, Moses makes himself more than a passive carrier of God's will—or, indeed, an uncompromising disciple—and instead part of a human process of law-making.[8]

If Michelangelo's *Moses* admits to the idea that human volition is fundamental to the administration of law and order, it also suggests that order is hard-wrought and bestowed with ambivalence. These concerns are taken up and developed throughout modernity: by the seventeenth and eighteenth century social contract theorists, and, later, in mid-twentieth century Hollywood Westerns.[9] They are illuminated further in detective fiction of the twentieth and twenty-first century, where the genre takes up this concern in such a way as to illuminate a further set of problems with social order. Here, suddenly, social order is something that can do more harm than good.

In this respect, we find post-1970s detective fiction extraordinarily prescient. After all, in the global north at least, so many of the pressing collective problems of the twenty-first century are related to social order: the difficulties in maintaining it, in trusting the guardians of it, and, more than anything else, the dangers in having either too little or too much of it. Politicians, journalists, and financiers, once responsible for maintaining liberal democracy, have been latterly recast in the popular imagination as criminals. Trust in state institutions and democratic processes has significantly waned across the economically-developed world in the aftermath of the 2008 economic crisis, as IPSOS'

Global Trends series demonstrates. Governments have responded to these problems of authority by extending criminal law, launching audits of the auditors, and making the work of state agencies more accessible to the public. What such measures fail to recognize is that the current crisis of social order is partly a problem of official control, oversight, and authority. If Michelangelo's *Moses* points towards this crisis by suggesting that human volition is a feature of social order, it is distinctively late modern social conditions that allow us to conceive of social order as humanly-conceived, the untrustworthy product of social hierarchies, neo-liberal politics, and institutional corruption.

This is a concern that lies at the heart of the post-1970s detective novel, where the implications of this deep distrust of social order tend to be vividly-sketched. The genre's interest in social order is, of course, nothing new. Indeed, since its emergence as a distinct literary genre in the mid-nineteenth century, the detective novel has been centrally concerned with the threat to social order from egotism, misanthropy, madness, and self-interest. Whilst these forces of chaos often converge within a single character, individual disorder is generally brought into focus through its relationship with the social in the detective novel. Evil is a *social* problem, in other words—in terms of its effect, if not origin—and the task of the detective is to keep it in abeyance. The quest, in the classic detective story formula at least, involves identifying, unveiling, and then sequestering evil to allow a return to order. Bertolt Brecht, in his essay on the popularity of the detective novel, draws a comparison between the detective and the crossword-puzzler (Brecht 2004: 90, originally 1938); both, he suggested, are dogmatically interested in sequential logic, in filling in the gaps until a satisfyingly complete picture is revealed. Perhaps even more intuitive—today, at least—is our association of the detective with the domestic help. The distinctive promise of the detective is that they react to things that can't be seen by the untrained human eye: they are attuned to microscopic abnormalities, to matter out of place. We talk of police detectives 'cleaning up' crime and 'putting away' criminals. We even use the same sing-song jingles as detergent adverts to capture crime as a social policy problem: say 'Tough on Crime, Tough on the Causes of Crime' several times, and see what it turns into.[10]

What is the point of the literary detective's cleaning? Siegfried Kracauer (in Frisby 1992) believed there to be a moral vacuum at the heart of the classic detective novel: here, he argued, the act of identifying 'who did this thing' becomes a good in and of itself and divorced from the thorny issues of responsibility and moral judgement—correlates, in his mind, of truth. The satisfaction derived from detective work, for Kracauer and Brecht at least, is the same as the satisfaction derived from completing the crossword puzzle: the characters fit into the established pattern, but there is no higher meaning to their ordering. A similar criticism might be made of the detective-as-cleaner. After all, tidying up, like doing a crossword puzzle, is a routine pursuit with no other end-goal than putting things into place. Or rather, it involves a continual process of putting things *back* into place according to a pre-established, unspoken but tacitly agreed-upon sense of where things belong. Like the cleaner, the detective is involved in locating and removing things that putrefy and disturb order—and, crucially, intrinsic to the job of both is the background knowledge that not everything can be cleaned, that some things are better off remaining hidden.

All of this is to suggest that literary detective-work is a more socially-meaningful and complex endeavour than Kracauer assumes. And in post-1970s detective fiction, it's an endeavour that involves a deep understanding of the basis and costs of social order. In most instances, this means that the task of detection cannot involve simply putting things back into place: it means, as well, considering the possibility that the status quo is the source of the problem. In these situations, justice is wrought with great difficulty—it is usually partial, and almost always requires violence. Above all, the literary detective faces a problem in locating responsibility: if the problem lies in structures of power, deeply entrenched, no single person is accountable. This was the argument of Chapter 3, and here we explored the idea that the old, dependable categories of blame and responsibility have become less clear-cut. One result of this is a loosening of moral boundaries. If no one individual is clearly responsible, then how do we confidently apportion blame? And if blame is diffuse, who should answer for a wrong-doing? The complicating factor in all of this is that the desire for someone to pay remains very much alive within the post-1970s detective novel and the world beyond. In fact, contemporary detective fiction is deeply concerned with the experience of victimisation, and the resulting pain, fear, and desire for vengeance.

This body of fiction offers a sort of compensation, one that raises further ethical questions about the nature of justice. We're thinking here of post-1970s detective fiction's revival of torture as a means of extracting the truth and vigilantism as a means of enacting justice.[11] It's notable that where contemporary detective fiction allows us the catharsis of apprehending a murderer, it is generally through his violent undoing, rather than arrest. This is surely partly because, in the world of post-1970s detective fiction, the law and its guardians are often unscrupulous and untrustworthy. Under these circumstances, arrest offers no guarantee that justice will be done. It's a concern that extends beyond the detective novel. In an era where most rapes recorded by the police fail to eventuate in a charge, and few then make it all the way to conviction, confidence in the criminal justice system is understandably low.[12] Post-1970s detective fiction answers to such frustrations and injustices, and it does so in such a way as to confirm that the old, prized ways of arriving at the truth and justice—so central to the task of building modern criminal justice—are outmoded and insufficient.

What we find in this body of fiction, then, is characters with a deep sense of injury, usually long-standing and accumulated over a lifecourse, and situations where crime is no longer a problem of discrete events and individual actors. In the background, and heavily implicated in the action, is a set of social conditions, recognizable to us as belonging to late modernity: sluggish, labyrinthine bureaucracies, the unassailable, invisible flights of capital, under-investment in public space, the ghettoization and gentrification of the city, and the hidden brutality of the domestic sphere. The resolution of these problems, as mentioned above, almost inevitably unleashes an elemental form of violence. The detective novel, in its finest form, does much to challenge this, or at least to raise questions about the rationality and ethics of answering horrifying violence with horrifying violence. One thing it makes startlingly clear is the lack of viable alternatives in responding to the problem of harm, when those who are victimized are powerless and those responsible so very powerful. In doing so, post-1970s detective fiction holds its readers to account, for at the same time as experiencing the short-term catharsis of a violent comeuppance, we surely recognise too that this is no answer to the bigger, more long-term problems detective novels place before us.

And here, again, we're brought back to the real world, because to feel vicariously the pinch of isolation and buried grievances is to see afresh the causes—and limitations—of rage, fear, and a desire for vengeance in the world beyond the detective novel. For one thing, it forces us to recognize that deep, unanswered anger goes somewhere. It is, we might say, a resource, one that can be channelled for nefarious ends, if it goes unrecognized and misunderstood. Post-1970s detective fiction refuses to remain silent on these matters. This body of fiction teaches us much, but this, we think, is its most important lesson.

Notes

1. In British sociology, the clearest expression of this argument is to be found in Savage and Burrows (2007) and Burrows and Savage (2014).
2. Even the Queen, in addressing a group of academics at the London School of Economists, bemoaned economics' failure to predict and pre-warn the events. In response, senior economists sent her a letter to explain the oversight (*The Guardian* 2009).
3. We're thinking here of, amongst other works, Goffman's (1990, originally 1956), *The Presentation of Self in Everyday Life* and Schutz's (1972, originally 1932), *The Phenomenology of the Social World.*
4. Much of Foucault's work is directed towards understanding how the line between the normative and pathological is drawn (notably, the volumes of *History of Sexuality*—Foucault 1998a, b). Bourdieu has a related concern. His work is centrally interested in how certain forms of consumption and cultural activity are connected to class positions, and variously valorised or maligned as a result (Bourdieu 2010, originally 1979). Bauman's interest in the pathological is different in kind, but clearly also central to his work: we're thinking, amongst other things, of his writing on the consumer society and exclusion (see Bauman 2007).
5. Detective fiction is a genre that is outside of the traditional literary canon. This has meant that, historically, at least, it has been

under-valued. For example, the work of Wilkie Collins—author of *The Moonstone*, one of the first detective novels—is less-studied and less highly-regarded than that of his peer Charles Dickens. The latter is regularly taken to be a cultural touchstone for Victorian London, whilst Collins' output tends to be categorised as melodrama, a style that has come to be understood pejoratively.

6. British sociology has been especially committed to the view that art is best understood as a cultural product that unconsciously expresses social relations. This is, of course, not without criticism from within mainstream sociology. Most notably, cultural sociology—largely a North American school of thought—seeks to set up a relationship between sociology and culture where culture is taken as important in and of itself (see Alexander 2003 for an overview of this approach, and McLennan 2005 for a critique). Our approach is distinct from each of these important schools of thought. Our aim has been to take up detective fiction's invitation to explore the problems of contemporary social life and follow up on its enquiries into the aberrant territory of the modern. We don't see literature as research material, but nor do we see it as belonging to a discrete cultural realm. Instead, we see it as akin to social theory.

7. See, for example, Donaldson's (2014) exploration of texture as a way of interpreting and evaluating film.

8. Freud's interpretation has been the subject of some debate in the Arts (see, for example, Bergstein 2006). One point of concern is whether Michelangelo's *Moses* in fact departs from the biblical account: for some, Moses is here portrayed in the moment before he dashes the tablets to the ground. We find Freud's interpretation convincing, but the more general point to make here is that, either way, the sculpture sets out to capture the role of human intention in law-making, our focus above.

9. Hobbes' *Leviathan*, published in 1651, is a classic early work of social contract theory, and is focussed on the need for the state to, on the one hand, guarantee law and order and, on the other, maintain individual freedom. The Hollywood Western, too, is centrally interested in how a balance is achieved between these two things. Bazin (1971) famously broached this issue in his essay on the Western, and saw the genre as working to mythologise the origin of the USA.

10. The phrase was famously used by Tony Blair, first in a 1993 article in the *New Statesman* as shadow Home Secretary, and again, in 1995,

in his second speech as leader at the Labour party conference. It is an important soundbite from this era of British politics, signalling, as it did, the birth of New Labour as a centre-ground political party, interested both in the causes of crime (a traditional concern of the left) and law and order (a traditional concern on the right).

11. There is a parallel here with state action in pursuing justice in the twenty-first century. We're thinking here of the increased public awareness concerning state reliance on torture, extraordinary rendition, and unilateral military action. It's violence that is of an entirely different character to that of the literary detective—one is the violence of the powerful, the other tends to be in the service of the oppressed—but what they both signal is a turn away from older methods of extracting truth and achieving justice.

12. Statistical data on rape recording and convictions is notoriously unreliable. One thing we do know is that there is a very significant amount of attrition at each stage of the criminal justice process. Most of the research in this area focuses on the situation in England and Wales, although Lovett and Kelly (2009) demonstrate that there is a Europe-wide trend towards increased atttition. To return to England and Wales, where the evidence is more substantial: here, police only record roughly a quarter of all crimes of rape reported to them (HMIC 2014a: 20). That's a very high rate of under-recording relative to other crime categories, as a 2014 report by Her Majesty's Inspectorate of Constabulary makes clear (HMIC 2014b). This isn't the only point at which cases 'fall out' of the system. Roughly 10% of the crimes that are recorded by the police are subsequently categorised as 'no-crimes', a higher rate of no-criming than for most other offences (HMIC 2014a: 22). And then less than a fifth of the cases that make it to the point of being referred to the Crown Prosecution Service are pursued further (HMIC 2014a: 25). And this, of course, is even before we get to the courtroom.

References

Alexander, J. 2003. *The Meanings of Social Life: A Cultural Sociology*. Oxford: Oxford University Press.

Bauman, Zygmunt. 2007. *Consuming Life*. Cambridge: Polity.

Bazin, Andre. 1971/2004. The Western, or the American Film Par Excellence. In *What Is Cinema?* Vol. I, ed. and trans. Gray. Berkeley: University of

California Press. Available at: https://archive.org/stream/Bazin_Andre_What_Is_Cinema_Volume_2/Bazin_Andre_What_Is_Cinema_Volume_2_djvu.txt. Accessed 14 May 2018.

Bergstein, Mary. 2006. Freud's Moses of Michelangelo: Vasari, Photography, and Art Historical Practice. *The Art Bulletin* 88 (1): 158–176. Available at: https://www.tandfonline.com/doi/abs/10.1080/00043079.2006.10786283. Accessed 14 May 2018.

Boltanski, Luc. 2014. *Mysteries and Conspiracies: Detective Stories, Spy Novels and the Making of Modern Societies*. Cambridge: Polity.

Bourdieu, Pierre. 2010 (originally 1979). *Distinction*. London: Routledge.

Brecht, Bertolt, Martin Harvey, and Aaron Kelly. 2004. On the Popularity of the Crime Novel. *The Irish Review* 31 (Spring/Summer): 90–95.

Burrows, R., and M. Savage. 2014. After the Crisis? Big Data and the Methodological Challenges of Empirical Sociology. *Sociology* (April–June): 1–6.

Donaldson, Lucy F. 2014. *Texture in Film*. London: Palgrave Macmillan.

Foucault, Michel. 1998a. *The History of Sexuality: The Will to Knowledge*, vol. 1. London: Penguin.

Foucault, Michel. 1998b. *The History of Sexuality: The Use of Pleasure*, vol. 2. London: Penguin.

Freud, Sigmund. 1914. The Moses of Michelangelo. In *Freud, The Standard Edition of the Complete Psychological Works*, vol. 13, ed. James Strachey, 211–236. London: Hogarth Press and the Institute of Psychoanalysis.

Frisby, David. 1992. Between the Spheres: Siegfried Krakauer and the Detective Novel. *Theory Culture, Society* 9 (1): 1–22.

Goffman, Erving. 1990 (originally 1956). *The Presentation of Self in Everyday Life*. London: Penguin.

HMIC. 2014a. *Rape Monitoring Group: Local Area Data for 2013/14*. London: HMSO. Available at: https://www.justiceinspectorates.gov.uk/hmicfrs/wp-content/uploads/staffordshire-rmg-digest-2013-14.pdf. Accessed 13 May 2018.

HMIC. 2014b. *Crime Recording: Making the Victim Count*. London: HMSO. Available at: https://www.justiceinspectorates.gov.uk/hmicfrs/wp-content/uploads/crime-recording-making-the-victim-count.pdf. Accessed 13 May 2018.

Lovett, Jo, and Liz, Kelly. 2009. *Different Systems, Similar Outcomes? Tracking Attrition in Reported Rape Cases Across Europe*. London: Child and Women Abuse Studies Unit.

McLennan, Gregor. 2005. The New American Cultural Sociology: An Appraisal. *Theory, Culture & Society* 22 (6): 1–18.

Savage, Mike, and Roger Burrows. 2007. The Coming Crisis of Empirical Sociology. *Sociology* 41 (5): 885–899. Available at: http://journals.sagepub.com/doi/abs/10.1177/0038038507080443. Accessed 13 May 2018.

Schutz, Alfred. 1972 (originally 1932). *The Phenomenology of the Social World*. Evanston, USA: Northwest University Press.

The Guardian. 25 July 2009. Senior Economists Sent Her a Letter to Explain the Oversight.

Appendices

Appendix A: Crime Writing Awards

Årets Lydbog, Sweden
Audible sounds of crime award
Buchliebling Austria
Coup de cœur de La Griffe Noire France
CrimeFest Awards
CWA Dagger in the Library
CWA Daggers
CWA Debut Dagger
CWA Diamond Dagger
CWA Gold Dagger
CWA Ian Fleming Steel Dagger
CWA John Creasey (New Blood) Dagger
Danskernes Yndlingsforfatter: Favourite Author Denmark
De beste thriller van het jaar Netherlands
De Gyldne Laurbær (The Golden Laurels), Denmark
Der Leserpreis die Besten Bücher Germany
eDunnit Award
Glasnøglen (The Glass Key), the Scandinavian crime award

© The Editor(s) (if applicable) and The Author(s) 2019
M. Evans et al., *Detecting the Social*, https://doi.org/10.1007/978-3-319-94520-0

Grand prix des Lectrices de Elle France
H.R.F. Keating Award
Harald Mogensen prisen Denmark
Honorary Craftsman Denmark
Krimi Blitz Award Germany
Læsernes Bogpris (Readers' Choice) Denmark
Le Prix d'honneur Boréales/Région Basse-Normandie du polar nordique France
MIMI-Preis: Booksellers and readers award Germany
Mystery Lover's Book of the Year: Crime Award USA
Prix des Lecteurs catégorie Polar France
Prix du Livre Robinsonnais France
Prix Plume du Thriller international/Plume d'Or France
The *Bord Gáis Energy* Irish Book Awards
The McIlvanney Prize:
The National (UK) Book Awards
The Petrona Award
The Ripper Award, Europe
The Sealed Room Award Japan
Theakston Old Peculier Crime Novel of The Yea

Appendix B: Detective and Crime Fiction Post 1970

Aaronovitch, Ben D
Adler-Olsen, Jussi
Alvtegen, Karen
Anwar, Amer
Atkinson, Kate
Bauer, Belinda
Billingham, Mark
Blædel, Sara
Booker, Simon
Bragi, Steinar
Bussi, Michel
Brookmyre, Christopher

Caan, Alex
Camilleri, Andrea Calogero
Carol, James
Claverton, Rosie
Cleeves, Ann
Cutts, Lisa
Downing, David
Duffy, Sean
Enger, Thomas
Farrell, Derek
Fossum, Karin
Fowler, Chris
Frank, Matthew
French, Tana
Galbraith, Robert
George, Elizabeth
Gilstrap, John
Gray, Alex
Green, Cass
Griffiths, Elly
Hall, M. R.
Hardie, Mark
Harper, Elodie
Harris, Oliver
Harvey, John
Hawley, Noah
Hayder, Mo
Hiekkapelto, Kati
Herron, Mick
Hilary, Sarah
Hill, Mark
Holliday, Susi
Holt, Anne
Horowitz, Anthony
Indriðason, Arnaldur
James, Peter

James, P.D.
Jónasson, Ragnar
Karolina, Anna
Kepler, Lars
Kerr, Philip
Kerridge, Jake
Khan, Vaseen
Läckberg, Camilla
Lapidus, Jens
Lemaitre, Pierre
Leon, Donna
Linksey, Howard
Lipska, Anna
Lönnaeus, Olle
Macbride, Stuart
Mackay, Malcolm
Maitland, Barry
Mark, David
Marklund, Lisa
Massie, Allan
Mankell, Henning
Marwood, Alex
McDermid, Val
McKinty, Adrian
McGown, Jill
McGrath, Melanie
Mina, Denise
De la Motte, Anders
Mukherjee, Abir
Meyrick, Denzil
Nesbø, Jo
Nesser, Håkan
Oswald, James
Phillips, Mike
Rankin, Ian
Rendell, Ruth

Robinson, Peter
Rowling, J. K.
Rudberg, Denise
Rydahl, Thomas
Sansom, C. J
Shaw, William
Sharp, Zoe
Sherez, Stav
Sigurðardóttir, Lilja
Sigurðardóttir, Yrsa
Spain, Jo
Sund, Axl Erik
Tantimedh, Adi
Taylor, Marshall
Theorin, Johan
Thomson, Lesley
Vargas, Fred
Villaros, Juan Pablo
Weaver, Tim
Westin, Gabriella
Whitaker, Chris
Yokoyama, Hideo

Afterword

Readers of this book may well have noticed that it has two authors and one editor, the latter with an encyclopaedic knowledge of detective fiction. Indeed, for one of the authors it has been precisely that range of information of authors and plots which has inspired the work on this book. This is just one of the many hidden, but essential features of co-thinking that has informed the production of this book. Another has been the work of discussing and agreeing the selection of novels. This Afterword attends to these matters. If, implicitly, this book claims that writing matters, that it can help us think, and that close, careful reading can be a means of critical enquiry, we think it's also useful to reflect upon the task of collaborative thinking and writing.

This point is made not just to (latterly!) introduce ourselves as authors of this book, and to set out here the importance, as we see it, of thinking about what it means to collaborate. We want to emphasise, too, that detective fiction asks us to enquire into the bases and nature of our collective existence. This book is a response to this invitation to engage with the unknown. Detective fiction brings together, through ties between individuals with different needs and aspirations (some murderous and criminal, others often of vulnerability and fragility) the social and the individual.

© The Editor(s) (if applicable) and The Author(s) 2019
M. Evans et al., *Detecting the Social*, https://doi.org/10.1007/978-3-319-94520-0

It shows—as it always has—the ways in which individual people are drawn into circumstances. But the crucial difference between detective fiction and mainstream fiction is that the social, the world outside the individual self, has a form and an identity. 'The social' lives and acts in detective fiction. More than that, it lives and acts *through* people, lives and acts *on* people. It is not just the background to our multiple subjectivities.

Just as we cannot (with no exceptions) have read every word of detective fiction, so we cannot know everything about the world in which we live. Detective fiction, we have argued, opens our eyes to many of the things about the contemporary world which many people would prefer not to think about: ruthless corporate greed, the corruption of individuals and institutions, forms of physical and emotional violence and the failure of the law to protect us from all these things. No one author of detective fiction does all these things, but *collectively* the genre does that. If we read post 1970s noir, be it about Hull or Helsinki, Belfast or Bergen we encounter varieties of these patterns, named and shamed by authors and fiction in ways which are seldom shared by either contemporary politics or the mainstream media. Of course, individual scandals attract attention, such as the Grenfell fire or the abuse of election funding in various European countries. But these tend to be regarded as single, separate events. As a collective body of fiction, detective novels ask us to work to see the connections between calamitous events and painful experiences. And it's worth noting here that individuals often read this fiction extensively. For those who are fans of the genre, reading means hopscotching across countries, police forces, and discrete cases. The result is a composite picture of what's going on.

'What's going on' was, incidentally, the working title of this book in its early stages. That came as much from our sense that detective novels had important answers to this question, as much as our belief that there was so much about today's social world that needed explaining. Over the past seven years we have met regularly to discuss (as eager readers) the latest detective novels we've read and explore (as professional sociologists) what's been happening socially and politically. Through this, the current book took shape, as we came to realise that the novels we were reading shed light on the extraordinary events unfolding in the real world—more so, we came to recognise, than mainstream sociology.

A note here, too, on the nature of those extraordinary 'real world' events that gave rise to the book. We started discussing the idea for this book during the summer of 2011, just after riots erupted in various UK cities. What followed, over the next seven years or so, is a catalogue of sociologically-fascinating events, which in turn came to form a tapestry as we discussed them alongside the novels we were reading. These events included the MP expenses scandal. The plan for private contractors to build and own a garden bridge crossing the Thames. The long-awaited results of the Hillsborough enquiry that finally offered formal exoneration to the football fans involved and clearly attributed blame to various official bodies. (And then, later, the news that there would be very few criminal prosecutions coming from the enquiry). Then came Brexit. And then Trump. And then *#MeToo*.

The composite picture—that phrase again, but it seems to us an important one—is of broken authority, unfettered corporatisation at odds with public need, and a deep public anger, born of the injury of neglect and disbelief, to which the snail-pace of official responses to crime offers a very weak answer. And so, as we have found in the second decade of the twenty-first century, people find other answers to an experience of powerlessness, answers that better attend to the depth of anger and the desire for change. This is the world that we find made piercingly, vividly real in detective fiction. And it's a world that we believe contemporary sociology should be more directly concerned with detailing and explicating.

These concerns touch our professional lives in more ways than one. All of us who have worked on this book are engaged, in different ways, with the social sciences, as they are taught and practised in UK universities. The changes to this institutional world have served, too, as the backdrop to this book, as our conversations have moved often seamlessly from discussing current affairs, to detective novels, to our professional milieu. We have seen the various forms of transformation which have produced greater and more invasive forms of competition into that sector. We have seen the impact of those changes on colleagues. In this limited way we have seen how institutional changes, made for political reasons, can make a difference to individual lives. We can detect the connection between the institutional and the personal. We have not seen (although universities have long been the sites of fictional murder) actual murder but we have seen various forms of the ways in which people are changed by having to work in circumstances which are not of their own choosing. The changes in universities are of course minor when compared by the various forms of diasporic events of the past two centuries, events of forced migration, two world wars, the deliberate attempt to annihilate cultures and growing forms of social inequality, but they constitute the more immediate history of the world in which we live.

This book has been intimately concerned with charting this near history of our social world and how we live. And to do so, we have returned and digested the novels that we believe do a particularly good job of crystallising these problems. So, we turn now to the question of how we selected these novels to discuss. As noted above, this has been at the heart of the collaborative process of writing this book: we have recommended books to one another, had books recommended to us by others, and thought together about novels' achievements and provocations. Through this, what started as a loose sense of which contributions sparked or fleshed out ideas became, over time, a more formal list of books and authors (see Appendices A and B). And as we began to write, the list underwent a further modification as we revisited it to consider whether there were books that we considered to be important (widely-read, award-winning, as well as rich, vivid accounts) that we'd omitted from the discussion, and whether that mattered. Those readers interested in methodological matters will possibly want to know here whether the books lead the argument, or the argument led the selection of books. The answer is that our list of core texts and argument grew together. We engaged one to revise and extend the other, and vice versa. When it has come to writing-up our ideas, though, not all of our core texts and authors have made into the main body of our argument. Attentive readers of detective fiction may also complain that we've missed novels pertinent to our argument. Both sets of omission are unavoidable, given that our purpose was to take up detective fiction's invitation to engage with the problems of the contemporary social world, rather than produce an encyclopaedia of detective novels.

And, as should be clear to any reader of this book, we have sought along the way to make a set of claims for recent detective fiction's achievements. We believe that this body of literature has been especially successful in capturing the intimate connections between the individual and society in such a way as to reveal the hard material reality of the world in which we live. It would, perhaps, be too ambitious to claim that detective fiction is *the* literary form which can render the reality of the twenty first century, but we could claim that it is more than able to detect many of its deep fissures. Several of those fissures are fundamental; all are recognised in detective fiction. One is the failure of various forms of the law (the legal system/ the police) to address both criminal and civil breaches of the law. The second is the failure of state institutions to protect the vulnerable, whether through deliberate policies of austerity or through the refusal to address abuse. The third, which will perhaps seem eccentric compared to previous points, is that of how we are to find pleasure and enjoyment in the twenty-first century. It is not accidental that many of the characters (criminal and otherwise) exist in various forms of various drug induced states. What alcohol is to an earlier generation, cocaine, and other hard drugs, are to more contemporary detectives and the people they are pursuing. We reject emphatically some version of the past in which happy (often poor) people gambled in Elysian fields, be they of classical mythology or the streets of towns and cities. Nevertheless, many detectives delight in that which the world seems to be unable to provide: thinking long and hard about what seems to be an intractable problem. Using your head is proposed throughout detective fiction as a form of real, lasting pleasure. Many times, we, as readers are invited to use our brains.

Using our brains has been a constant delight in this project. It has been a real joy to work with others (often an under-valued opportunity in the social sciences and the humanities). It has also been a real pleasure—if sometimes deeply unsettling and disturbing—to encounter worlds outside our own. To see the murderers not as the pursued but as part of the world in which we live. To observe the world beyond its accepted and endorsed forms. To use and encounter imaginations in ways which do not have to return to the past or invent a fictional future. We hope that you have shared these pleasures.

Bibliography

Adler-Olsen, Jussi. *Mercy*. 2011. London: Penguin.

Adorno, Theodor, and Max Horkheimer. 1977 (originally 1944). *Dialectic of Enlightenment*. London: Verso.

Ahmed, Sara. 2013. *The Cultural Politics of Emotion*. London: Routledge.

Alexander, J. 2003. *The Meanings of Social Life: A Cultural Sociology*. Oxford: Oxford University Press.

Alvtegen, Karin. 2003. *Missing*. UK: Felony and Mayhem.

Arvaas, P., and A. Nestingen. 2011. *Scandinavian Crime Fiction*. Cardiff: University of Wales Press.

Åström, B., K. Gregersdotter, and T. Horeck (eds.). 2012. *Rape in Stieg Larsson's Millennium Trilogy and Beyond: Contemporary Scandinavian and Anglophone Crime Fiction*. Basingstoke: Palgrave Macmillan. Available at: https://www.palgrave.com/gb/book/9780230308404#aboutBook. Accessed 14 May 2018.

Auden, Wystan Hugh. 1948. The Guilty Vicarage: Notes on the Detective Story, by an Addict. *Harper's*, May, 406–412.

Auden, Wystan Hugh. 1963. The Guilty Vicarage. In *The Dyer's Hand*. London: Faber and Faber.

Austen, Jane. 1833. *Mansfield Park: A Novel*. London: Richard Bentley.

Baker, Tom, and Jonathan Simon. 2002. *Embracing Risk: The Changing Culture of Insurance and Responsibility*. Chicago, IL: University of Chicago Press.

© The Editor(s) (if applicable) and The Author(s) 2019
M. Evans et al., *Detecting the Social*, https://doi.org/10.1007/978-3-319-94520-0

Baudrillard, Jean. 1994. *Simulacra and Simulation*. Ann Arbor: University of Michigan Press.

Baudrillard, Jean. 1995. *The Gulf War Did Not Take Place*. Bloomington: Indiana University Press.

Bauman, Zygmunt. 1992. *Intimations of Postmodernity*. London: Routledge.

Bauman, Zygmunt. 2007. *Consuming Life*. Cambridge: Polity.

Bazin, Andre. 1971/2004. The Western, or the American Film Par Excellence. In *What Is Cinema?* Vol. I, ed. and trans. Gray. Berkeley: University of California Press. Available at: https://archive.org/stream/Bazin_Andre_What_Is_Cinema_Volume_2/Bazin_Andre_What_Is_Cinema_Volume_2_djvu.txt. Accessed 14 May 2018.

Benjamin, Walter. 1970. Theses on the Philosophy of History. In *Illuminations*. London: Cape.

Benjamin, Walter. 2002. *The Arcades Project*. Cambridge, MA: Harvard University Press. Available at: http://traumawien.at/stuff/workshops/language-as-materials/benjamin-_walter_-_the_arcades_project.pdf. Accessed 14 May 2018.

Benjamin, Walter, Martin Harvey, and Aaron Kelly. 2004. Travelling with Crime Novels. *The Irish Review* 31 (Spring–Summer): 88–89.

Bergman, Kerstin. 2014. *Swedish Crime Fiction: The Making of Nordic Noir*. Milan: Mimesis International.

Bergstein, Mary. 2006. Freud's Moses of Michelangelo: Vasari, Photography, and Art Historical Practice. *The Art Bulletin* 88 (1): 158–176. Available at: https://www.tandfonline.com/doi/abs/10.1080/00043079.2006.10786283. Accessed 14 May 2018.

Berlant, Lauren Gail. 2011. *Cruel Optimism*. Durham: Duke University Press.

Best, Joel. 1999. *Random Violence: How We Talk about New Crimes and Victims*. Berkeley: University of California Press.

Beveridge, William. 1942. *Social Insurance and Allied Services*—Beveridge Report of 1942. Available at: https://www.sochealth.co.uk/national-health-service/public-health-and-wellbeing/beveridge-report/. Accessed 14 May 2018.

Bew, John. 2017. *Citizen Clem: A Biography of Attlee*. Oxford: Oxford University Press.

Blair, Tony. 1993. Tony Blair Is Tough on Crime, Tough on the Causes of Crime. *New Statesman*, January 29, 1991. Available at: https://www.newstatesman.com/2015/12/archive-tony-blair-tough-crime-tough-causes-crime. Accessed 12 May 2018.

Blair, Tony. 1995. Leader's Speech, Brighton Party Conference, 1995. Available at: http://www.britishpoliticalspeech.org/speech-archive.htm?speech=201.

Bloch, Ernst. 1988. A philosophical View of the Detective Novel. *The Utopian Function of Art and Literature*, 245–264. London: MIT Press.

Boltanski, Luc. 2006. *The New Spirit of Capitalism*. London: Verso.

Boltanski, Luc. 2014. *Mysteries and Conspiracies: Detective Stories, Spy Novels and the Making of Modern Societies*. Cambridge: Polity.

Bourdieu, Pierre. 2010 (originally 1979). *Distinction*. London: Routledge.

Box, Steve. 1971. *Deviance, Reality and Society*. New York: Holt, Rinehart and Winston.

Brecht, Bertolt, Martin Harvey, and Aaron Kelly. 2004. On the Popularity of the Crime Novel. *The Irish Review* 31 (Spring/Summer): 90–95.

Burrows, R., and M. Savage. 2014. After the Crisis? Big Data and the Methodological Challenges of Empirical Sociology. *Sociology* (April–June): 1–6.

Calder, Angus. 1971. *The People's War*. London: Panther.

Chandler, Raymond. 1988 (originally 1944). The Simple Art of Murder. In *The Simple Art of Murder*, ed. R. Chandler, 1–18. New York: Vintage.

Christie, Agatha. 1921. *The Mysterious Affair at Styles*. London: Bodley Head.

Churchill, David. 2016. Security and Visions of the Criminal: Technology, Professional Criminality and Social Change in Victorian and Edwardian Britain. *British Journal of Criminology* 56 (5): 857–876.

Clark, Tom, and Anthony Heath. 2014. *Hard Times: Inequality, Recession, Aftermath*. London and New Haven: Yale University Press.

Collins, Wilkie. 1985 (originally 1868). *The Moonstone*. London: Everyman Paperbacks.

Cornwell, Patricia Daniels. 1998. *A Scarpetta Omnibus: Three Novels in One Volume*. London: Little, Brown.

Critcher, Chas. 2010. Media, Government, and Moral Panic: The Politics of Paedophilia in Britain 2000–1. *Journalism Studies* 3 (4): 521–535.

Crook, John A. 1976. *Law and Life of Rome: 90 B.C.–A.D. 212*. Ithaca, NY: Cornell University Press.

Crozier, Michel, Samuel Huntington, and Joji Watanuki. 1975. *The Crisis of Democracy: Report on the Governmentality of the Democracies to the Trilateral Commission*. New York: New York University Press.

Cutts, Lisa. 2014. *Remember, Remember*. London: Simon and Schuster.

De Quincey, Thomas. 2015 (originally 1827). *On Murder Considered as One of the Fine Arts; Being an Address Made to a Gentleman's Club Concerning its Aesthetic Appreciation*. London: Penguin.

Deborah, Crombie. 2017. *The Garden of Lamentations*. New York: HarperCollins.

Delaney, Shelagh. 1959. *A Taste of Honey*. London: Grove Press.

Deleuze, Gilles. 2004. The Philosophy of Crime Novels. In *Desert Islands and Other Texts 1953–1974*. Paris: Semiotext(e).

Dibdin, Michael. 1998. *The Aurelio Zen Omnibus*. London: Faber and Faber.

Dolan, Eva. 2014. *Long Way Home*. London: Harvill Secker.

Donaldson, Lucy F. 2014. *Texture in Film*. London: Palgrave Macmillan.

Dorling, Danny. 2014. *Inequality and the 1%*. London: Verso.

Douglas, Mary. 2003 (originally 1966). *Purity and Danger: An Analysis of Concepts of Pollution and Taboo*. London: Routledge.

Effron, Malcah (ed.). 2013. *The Millennial Detective: Essays on Trends in Crime Fiction, Film and Television*. Jefferson, NC: McFarland.

Ehrenreich, Barbara. 1989. *Fear of Falling: The Inner Life of the Middle Class*. New York: Knopf.

Ellwood, Charles A. 1912. Lombroso's Theory of Crime. *Journal of Criminal Law and Criminology* 2 (5): 716–723.

Emsley, Clive. 2005. *Crime and Society in England 1750–1900*, 3rd ed. Harlow, UK: Longman.

Erikson, Richard V., and Aaron Doyle (eds.). 2003. *Risk and Morality*. Toronto: University of Toronto Press.

Eriksson, Kjell. 2011. *The Demon of Dakar*. London: Allison and Busby.

Flaubert, Gustave. 1857. *Madame Bovary: Moeurs de province*. Vienne: Mainz.

Flynn, Gillian. 2012. *Gone Girl*. London: Phoenix.

Foreman, James. 2017. *Locking Up Our Own: Crime and Punishment in Black America*. New York: Farrar, Straus and Giroux.

Forrester, Andrew. 2015 (originally 1864). *The Female Detective*. London: The British Library.

Forshaw, Barry. 2012. *Death in a Cold Climate: A Guide to Scandinavian Crime Fiction*. Basingstoke: Palgrave Macmillan.

Forshaw, Barry (ed.). 2016. *Detective*. Bristol and Chicago: Intellect.

Fossum, Karin. 2004. *The Murder of Harriet Krohn*. Boston, MA: Houghton Mifflin Harcourt.

Foucault, Michel. 1991. *Discipline and Punish: The Birth of the Prison*. London: Penguin.

Foucault, Michel. 1998a. *The History of Sexuality: The Will to Knowledge*, vol. 1. London: Penguin.

Foucault, Michel. 1998b. *The History of Sexuality: The Use of Pleasure*, vol. 2. London: Penguin.

Frank, Parkin. 1968. *Middle Class Radicalism*. Manchester: Manchester University Press.

Frank, Matthew. 2014. *If I Should Die*. London: Penguin.

French, Tana. 2012. *Broken Harbour*. London: Hodder and Stoughton.

Freud, Sigmund. 1914. The Moses of Michelangelo. In *Freud, The Standard Edition of the Complete Psychological Works*, vol. 13, ed. James Strachey, 211–236. London: Hogarth Press and the Institute of Psychoanalysis.

Friedan, Betty. 1963. *The Feminine Mystique*. New York: W. W. Norton.

Frisby, David. 1992. Between the Spheres: Siegfried Krakauer and the Detective Novel. *Theory Culture, Society* 9 (1): 1–22.

Furedi, Frank. 2002. *The Culture of Fear*. London and New York: Continuum.

Furedi, Frank. 2003. *Therapy Culture: Cultivating Vulnerability in an Uncertain Age*. London: Routledge.

Gadda, Carlo Emilio. 1965 (originally 1957). *That Awful Mess on the Via Merulana*, trans. William Weaver. London and New York: NYRB.

García-Moreno, Claudia, and Christina Pallitto. 2013. *Global and Regional Estimates of Violence Against Women: Prevalence and Health Effects of Intimate Partner and Non-partner Violence*. Geneva: World Health Organisation.

Gardner, Jane F. 2009. *Women in Roman Law and Society*. London: Routledge.

Gerritsen, Tess. 2007. *Vanish* (Rizzoli & Isles series 5). London and New York: Bantam Books.

Giddens, Anthony. 1990. *The Consequences of Modernity*. Cambridge: Polity Press.

Godwin, William. 1794. *Things as They Are or, the Adventures of Caleb Williams*. London. Available at: http://public-library.uk/ebooks/18/42.pdf. Accessed 13 May 2018.

Goffman, Erving. 1990 (originally 1956). *The Presentation of Self in Everyday Life*. London: Penguin.

Gregersdotter, Katarina. 2016/2015. Detective Martin Beck. In *Crime Uncovered: Detective*, ed. Barry Forshaw, 44–55. Bristol and Chicago: Intellect Books.

Gregoriou, Christiana. 2007. *Deviance in Contemporary Crime Fiction*. Basingstoke: Palgrave Macmillan.

Grimstad, Paul, 2016. What Makes Great Detective Fiction: According to T. S. Eliot. *The New Yorker*, February 2.

Harvey, David. 2005. *A Brief History of Neo-liberalism*. Oxford: Oxford University Press.

Harvey, John. 2004. *Flesh & Blood (Frank Elder #1)*. London: Carroll & Graf Publishers.

Harvey, John. 2008. *Cold in Hand*. London: Carroll & Graf Publishers.

Heelas, Paul, Scott Lash, and Paul Morris (eds.). 1995. *Detraditionalization*. Oxford: Wiley-Blackwell.

Herron, Mick. 2010. *Slow Horses*. London: Soho Crime.

Herzog, Todd. 2009. *Crime Stories: Criminalistic Fantasy and the Culture of Crisis in Weimar Germany*. USA: Berghahn Books.

Hilliard, Chris. 2017. *The Littlehampton Libels: A Miscarriage of Justice and a Mystery about Words in 1920s England*. Oxford: Oxford University Press.

HMIC. 2014a. *Rape Monitoring Group: Local Area Data for 2013/14*. London: HMSO. Available at: https://www.justiceinspectorates.gov.uk/hmicfrs/wp-content/uploads/staffordshire-rmg-digest-2013-14.pdf. Accessed 13 May 2018.

HMIC. 2014b. *Crime Recording: Making the Victim Count*. London: HMSO. Available at: https://www.justiceinspectorates.gov.uk/hmicfrs/wp-content/uploads/crime-recording-making-the-victim-count.pdf. Accessed 13 May 2018.

Hobbes, Thomas. 2014 (originally 1651). *Leviathan*. Ware, UK: Wordsworth Editions.

Hobsbawm, Eric J. 1994. *Age of Extremes: A Short History of the Twentieth Century*. London: Michael Joseph.

Høeg, Peter. 1993. *Miss Smilla's Feeling for Snow*. UK: Farrar, Straus and Giroux Inc. and the Harvill Press.

Horowitz, Anthony. 2017. *The Word Is Murder*. London: Century.

Hughes, G., and G. Lewis. 1998. *Unsettling Welfare: The Reconstruction of Social Policy*. London: Routledge.

Indriðason, Arnaldur. 2014. *Oblivion*. London: Vintage.

Inglehart, Ronald F. 1990. *Culture Shift in Advanced Industrial Society*. Princeton, NJ: Princeton University Press.

Jenkins, P. 1998. *Moral Panic: Changing Concepts of the Child Molester in Modern America*. New Haven, CT: Yale University Press.

Jones, M. 2016. A Room Going Spare: Lodgers, Nannies, and Strangers in the Home. In *Spaces of the Cinematic Home: Behind the Screen Door*, ed. E. Andrews, S. Hockenhull, and F. Pheasant-Kelly, 167–179. London: Routledge.

Lacey, N. 2012. *Women, Crime, and Character: From Moll Flanders to Tess of the D'Urbervilles*. Oxford: Oxford University Press.

Lapidus, Jens. 2013. *Never Screw Up*. London: Pan.

Lapidus, Jens. 2014a. *Easy Money*. London: Pan.

Lapidus, Jens. 2014b. *Life Deluxe*. London: Pan.

Le Cheminant, Wayne, and John M. Parnish (eds.). 2011. *Manipulating Democracy: Democratic Theory, Political Psychology and the Mass Media*. London and New York: Routledge.

Lees, Loretta. 2001. *The Emancipatory City: Paradoxes and Possibilities*. London: Sage.

Lenman, Bruce, and Geoffrey Parker. 1980. The State, the Community and the Criminal Law in Early Modern Europe. In *Crime and the Law: the Social History of Crime in Western Europe Since 1500*, ed. V.A.C. Gatrell, B. Lenman, and G. Parker. London: Europa Publications.

Leovy, Jill. 2015. *Ghettoside: Investigating a Homicide Epidemic*. New York: Spiegel.

Lewis, Michael. 2010. *The Big Short*. London: Penguin.

Lofland, Lyn H. 1973. *A World of Strangers: Order and Action in Urban Public Space*. New York: Basic Books.

Lovett, Jo, and Liz, Kelly. 2009. *Different Systems, Similar Outcomes? Tracking Attrition in Reported Rape Cases Across Europe*. London: Child and Women Abuse Studies Unit.

Lyotard, Jean-François. 1984 (originally 1979). *The Postmodern Condition: A Report on Knowledge*. Manchester: Manchester University Press.

Mankell, Henning. 2012. *The White Lioness*. London: Vintage.

Mankell, Henning. 2003. *Firewall*. UK: The Harvill Press.

Marcuse, Herbert. 1965. A Critique of Pure Tolerance. In *A Critique of Pure Tolerance*, ed. Robert Paul Wolff, Barrington Moore, Jr., and Herbert Marcuse. Boston, MA: Beacon Press.

Mark, David. 2012. *The Dark Winter*. London: Quercus.

Marsh, Ngaio. 2018. *Money in the Morgue: The New Inspector Alleyn Novel*. London: Collins Crime Club.

Martin, Jane. 2008. Beyond Suffrage: Feminism, Education and the Politics of Class in the Inter-war Years. *British Journal of the Sociology of Education* 29 (4): 411–423.

Marx, Gary T. 2016. *Windows into the Soul: Surveillance and Society in an Age of Technology*. Chicago: Chicago University Press.

Massie, Allan. 2010. *Death in Bordeaux*. London: Quartet Books.

McIlvanney, William. 1977. *Laidlaw*. London: Hodder and Stoughton.
McIlvanney, William. 1983. *The Papers of Tony Veitch*. London: Hodder and Stoughton.
McIlvanney, William. 1991. *Strange Loyalties*. London: Hodder and Stoughton.
McKinty, Adrian. 2012. *The Cold Cold Ground*. London: Serpent's Tail.
McLennan, Gregor. 2005. The New American Cultural Sociology: An Appraisal. *Theory, Culture & Society* 22 (6): 1–18.
Miller, Keith. 2012. Review of Capital by John Lanchester. *The Daily Telegraph*, February 23.
Mitchell, Gladys. 1929. *The Mystery of the Butcher's Shop*. London: Gollancz.
Mitchell, Gladys. 1932. *The Saltmarsh Murders*. London: Gollancz.
Moretti, Franco. 1983. 'Clues' in Franco Moretti, *Signs Taken for Wonders: Essays in the Sociology of Literary Forms*, 130–156. London: Verso.
Nesbø, Jo. 2006. *The Redbreast*. New York: Harvill Secker.
Offer, Avner. 2006. *The Challenge of Affluence*. Oxford: Oxford University Press.
Orwell, George. 1946. The Decline of the English Murder. *Tribune*, February 15.
Paretsky, Sara. 1982. *Indemnity Only*. London: Hodder and Stoughton.
Peacock, S. (ed.). 2013. *Stieg Larsson's Millennium Trilogy: Interdisciplinary Approaches to Nordic Noir in Page and Screen*. Basingstoke: Palgrave Macmillan.
Peacock, Steven. 2014. *Swedish Crime Fiction: Novel, Film, Television*. Manchester: Manchester University Press.
Poe, Edgar Allen. Originally 1841. The Murder in the Rue Morgue. *Grahams Magazine*, New York. Reprinted in Edgar Allan Poe. 1927. *Collected Works of Edgar Allan Poe*. New York: Walter J. Black.
Powell, Jonathan. 2014. *Talking to Terrorists: How to End Armed Conflicts*. London: Bodley Head.
Rabin, Dana Y. 2004. *Identity, Crime, and Legal Responsibility in Eighteenth Century England*. Basingstoke: Palgrave Macmillan.
Rankin, Ian. 1996. *Let It Bleed*. London: Orion.
Reichs, Kathy. Tempe Brennan series, see https://www.goodreads.com/series/43556-temperance-brennan. Accessed 13 May 2018.
Reiner, Robert. 2010. *The Politics of the Police*. Oxford: Oxford University Press.
Roseneil, Sasha. 1995. *Disarming Patriarchy: Feminism and Political Action at Greenham Common*. Buckingham: Open University Press.
Roussel, V. 2003. New Moralities of Risk and Political Responsibility. In *Risk and Morality*, ed. R. Ericson, 117–144. Toronto: University of Toronto Press.
Rydahl, Thomas. 2016. *The Hermit*. UK: Point Blank.
Sansom, Christopher John. 2003. *Dissolution*. London: Macmillan.

Savage, Mike, and Roger Burrows. 2007. *The Coming Crisis of Empirical Sociology. Sociology* 41 (5): 885–899. Available at: http://journals.sagepub.com/doi/abs/10.1177/0038038507080443. Accessed 13 May 2018.

Schutz, Alfred. 1972 (originally 1932). *The Phenomenology of the Social World.* Evanston,USA: Northwest University Press.

Scraggs, John. 2005. *Crime Fiction.* London: Routledge.

Sennett, Richard. 1993. *The Fall of Public Man.* London: Faber and Faber.

Shaw, William. 2013. *A Song from Dead Lips.* London: Quercus.

Shaw, William. 2014. *A House of Knives.* London: Quercus.

Shaw, William. 2015. *A Book of Scars.* London: Quercus.

Shaw, William. 2017. *Sympathy for the Devil.* London: Quercus.

Shelley, Mary. 1818. *Frankenstein: Or, the Modern Prometheus.* London.

Sherez, Stav. 2013. *Eleven Days.* London: Faber.

Sigmund, Anna Maria. 2000. *Women of the Third Reich.* Ontario: NDA Publishing.

Sigurðardóttir, Yrsa. 2010. *Ashes to Dust* (Book 3 of 6 in the Þóra Guðmundsdóttir Series). London: Hodder.

Sillitoe, Alan. 1959. *The Loneliness of the Long-Distance Runner.* London: W. H. Allen.

Sillitoe, Alan. 1958. *Saturday Night and Sunday Morning.* London: W. H. Allen.

Simmel, Georg. 1978. The Mobilisation of Values. In *The Philosophy of Money.* London: Routledge.

Sjöwall, Maj, and Per Wahlöö. 2007. *The Man on the Balcony.* London: Harper Perennial.

Stedman-Jones, Daniel. 2012. *Masters of the Universe.* Princeton: Princeton University Press.

Summerfield, Penny, and Corinna Peniston-Bird. 2007. *Contesting Home Defence: Men, Women and the Home Guard in the Second World War.* Manchester: Manchester University Press.

Summerfield, Penny. 2014. *Women Workers in the Second World War.* London: Routledge.

Sund, Erik Axl. 2016. *The Crow Girl.* London: Penguin.

Tapper, Michael. 2014. *Swedish Cops: From Sjöwall and Wahlöö to Stieg Larsson.* Bristol and Chicago: Intellect.

Taylor, Ian, Paul Walton, and Jock Young. 1973. *The New Criminology: For a Social Theory of Deviance.* London: Routledge.

Taylor, Charles. 2013. *Margaret Thatcher: The Authorised Biography*, vol. 1. London: Allen Lane.

Taylor, Nicole. 2017. *Three Girls*, miniseries directed by Phillipa Lowthorpe, May 16–18, 2017. London: BBC Studios and Studio Lambert. Available at: https://www.bbc.co.uk/programmes/b08rgd5n. Accessed 13 May 2018.

Tey, Josephine. 1951. *The Daughter of Time*. London: Peter Davies.

The Guardian. 2009a. This Is How We Let the Credit Crunch Happen, Ma'am…. Sunday July 26. Available at: https://www.theguardian.com/uk/2009/jul/26/monarchy-credit-crunch. Accessed 13 May 2018.

The Guardian. 2009b. Senior Economists Sent Her a Letter to Explain the Oversight.

Thomas, Keith. 1971. *Religion and the Decline of Magic*. Harmondsworth: Penguin.

Thomas, Lyn. 1995. In Love with Inspector Morse. *Feminist Review* 51 (Autumn). Available at: https://link.springer.com/article/10.1057/fr.1995.30. Accessed 13 May 2018.

Todd, Selina. 2015. *The People: The Rise and Fall of the Working Class*. London: John Murray.

Upson, Nicola. 2008. *An Expert in Murder*. London: Faber and Faber.

Urwick, Edward J. 1912. *A Philosophy of Social Progress*. London: Methuen. Available at: https://archive.org/details/philosophyofsoci00urwiuoft. Accessed 13 May 2018.

Voltaire (François-Marie Arouet). 1748. *Zadig*. Available at: https://www.ebooksgratuits.com/blackmask/voltaire_zadig.pdf or https://www.gutenberg.org/files/18972/18972-h/18972-h.htm. Accessed 13 May 2018.

Watt, Ian. 1957. *The Rise of the Novel*. London: Chatto and Windus.

Woolf, Virginia. 1938. *Three Guineas*. London: Hogarth Press.

Worsley, Peter. 1969. *The Third World*. London: Weidenfeld and Nicolson.

Index

© The Editor(s) (if applicable) and The Author(s) 2019
M. Evans et al., *Detecting the Social*, https://doi.org/10.1007/978-3-319-94520-0